UK Ninja Dual Zone
Air Fryer Cookbook

2023-2024

1900 Days of Simple, Crispy, Healthy Recipes with Expert Tips & Tricks for Beginners | Unveiling the Mystery of the Dual Zone Air Fryer

Martha K. Frederick

Contents

INTRODUCTION

Your Ultimate Guide to the Ninja Dual Zone Air Fryer

As a chef and mom of two, I have had the pleasure of experimenting and exploring the capabilities of the newest kitchen appliances on the market. In this cookbook, I will share with you my experience with the Ninja Dual Zone Air Fryer. I must admit at the very beginning, this is not an average kitchen gadget. In fact, this is a high-powered tool that allows me to fry, reheat, bake, roast, and dehydrate a wide range of dishes in a fraction of the time. Plus, it requires little to no oil! With its dual-zone technology, perfectly crispy and flavorful meals become a reality! The Dual Zone technology has drastically changed the way I prepare my meals – they are much better and healthier!

Whether you are a beginner or a seasoned cook, the Ninja Dual Zone Air Fryer will quickly become your best culinary companion. Trust me, it is a godsend! With two separate drawers, I can cook two different meals simultaneously, making cooking a breeze. It's like having an oven and air fryer in one, or two air fryers. The results? Culinary masterpiece every time. Meal prep and family gatherings become more enjoyable with the Ninja Dual Zone Air Fryer! Whether it's a batch of chips or a pile of doughnuts, the capabilities of this kitchen gadget are impressive. And the best part? You can enjoy your restaurant favourites with only a fraction of the oil. What more could we ask for?

Are you ready to embark on a culinary adventure with the UK Ninja Dual Zone Air Fryer? Join me and discover the best tips and tricks for using the Ninja Dual Zone Air Fryer! My cookbook embraces numerous cuisine styles, from old-fashioned meals to the newest culinary trends. I have included a wide variety of recipes that will inspire and excite you in so many ways. My Ninja Foodi Dual Zone Cookbook includes a wide range of baked and fried meals, from satisfying family delicacies and easy appetizers to delectable desserts. Every recipe includes a list of ingredients, step-by-step instructions, estimated cooking time and number of servings. Further, there are a lot of useful tricks and tips that I have learned along the way. Plus, I've also included nutritional facts of every dish, while optional ingredients aren't included in the nutritive analysis. Learn how to cook your favourite fried foods in this revolutionary Air Fryer and achieve stellar results every time!

Getting Started: The Basics

If you're a home cook looking to make your cooking healthier and more convenient, the Ninja Foodi Dual Zone Air Fryer is the answer. Before diving into this magical world of air frying, it's good to familiarize yourself with the basics of the Ninja Dual Zone Air Fryer. Here are some major points to keep in mind:

- **Dual-Zone Cooking.** This cutting-edge technology allows you to cook two different foods simultaneously. You can prepare a complete meal for your family by cooking a main course and a side dish in one Air Fryer. Fish and chips in one go? No problem, the Ninja Dual Zone Air Fryer will save you time and energy! With these versatile cooking options, you can cook your favourite fried foods in your own kitchen. The result is a crispy, golden perfection!

As an Air Fryer, the Ninja Foodi uses powerful convection heating to circulate hot air around your food. This technology allows it to cook quickly and evenly, reducing the need for excessive oil.

- **Temperature and Time Control.** One of the main features of the Ninja Dual Zone Air Fryer is its precise temperature and time control. You can have control over the process thanks to customizable cooking times. The digital display and one-touch controls simplify the cooking process, so you can set time and temperature parameters according to your recipe or your personal preferences. Lovely!

- **Five Cooking Options.** You can air fry, bake, roast, dehydrate and reheat your food in the Ninja Dual Zone Air Fryer. In my opinion, this is a vast array of cooking options. Each ingredient requires a specific temperature and cooking. Make use of the dual-zone technology by using "MATCH" and "SYNC" options. In this way, you can optimize the cooking process and ensure everything is ready at the same time. Let your culinary imagination run wild!

Here are three main benefits of the Ninja Dual Zone Air Fryer:

- **Healthier Meals.** Compared to traditional frying methods, the Ninja Dual Zone Air Fryer offers a healthier alternative. By using up to 75% less oil, you can enjoy crispy and delicious dishes without soaking your food in oil. No oil, no guilt! Additionally, the even and consistent cooking provided by this technology ensures that your food is cooked to perfection, every time. The Ninja Dual Zone Air Fryer will crisp up foods like chicken wings, veggies and fish, giving them that delicious crispiness without the added calories and unhealthy fats. I love to enjoy my food without sacrificing taste and texture. How about you?
- **Time and Cost Efficiency.** This incredible machine cooks your food faster than conventional ovens. In general, Air Fryers preheat faster than ovens, which can save energy in the long run. It is effective when it comes to meal prep and batch cooking, too.
- **Versatility.** The Ninja Dual Zone Air Fryer goes beyond air frying. Baking, roasting, and dehydrating become easy and convenient with this revolutionary kitchen appliance. The Ninja Dual Zone Air Fryer is suitable for a wide range of dishes, from easy breakfast omelettes and succulent meats to perfectly baked pastries. This tool will save you time and counter space. It's time to unleash your creativity with the Ninja Dual Zone Air Fryer!

How to Clean the Ninja Dual Zone Air Fryer?

Regular cleaning of any kitchen appliance, including the Ninja Dual Zone Air Fryer, is essential. Your machine can accumulate food particles, odors, and grease over time, so these residues can affect its optimal performance.

- **Cleaning the Exterior.** Simply wipe it down with a damp sponge or cloth. For stubborn stains, you can use a mild dish soap solution. Do not use harsh chemicals and abrasive cleaners; otherwise, you can damage the finish. Make sure to dry the exterior thoroughly before storing your Ninja Dual Zone Air Fryer.
- **Cleaning the Cooking Basket, Drawers, and Crisper Plates.** These components come into direct contact with your food, so it's crucial to keep them in good condition. Begin by removing all these elements from your Ninja Dual Zone Air Fryer. Remove any food debris and then, soak them in warm soapy water for about 10 minutes. This simple trick will lose any stuck-on residue. Use a sponge or brush to scrub away the residue. Rinse the components thoroughly and dry them completely.
- **Cleaning the Heating Elements.** This is crucial for optimal performance. How to do that? First and foremost, make sure your machine is unplugged and completely cool. Now, remove any loose debris using a soft cloth. Avoid submerging the heating elements in the water.

In addition to regular cleaning, here are some extra tips to keep your Ninja Dual Zone Air Fryer in top condition:

- Check the user manual for any specific cleaning instructions or recommendations from the manufacturer.
- If there are stubborn stains or residue, use a mixture of vinegar and water and gently wipe the components.
- Clean your Ninja Dual Zone Air Fryer after each use to prevent the buildup of hardened food residues. Regular maintenance will not only ensure its longevity but also keep your food tasting great every time.
- Do not use metal items that can scratch the non-stick surface.

Possible Risks of Using the Ninja Dual Zone Air Fryer

Having used this incredible machine for several years now, I can say that it has become one of the best kitchen companions ever. However, I am aware of the potential risks associated with using the Ninja Dual Zone Air Fryer.

- **The Risk of Overcooking or Undercooking.** Follow instructions and do not leave your food in the cooking basket for too long. This can result in dry and overcooked meals. The same applies to undercooked food. So, I always closely monitor my food while it's cooking and follow the recommended cooking times and temperatures. To minimize the risk of uneven cooking, flip the food halfway through the cooking process, cut larger food items into smaller pieces, and use the appropriate accessories. It is important to experiment with air frying and over time, you will find this perfect balance between crispiness and juiciness.
- **The Risk of Health Hazards.** In general, air frying is considered a healthier alternative to deep frying, However, one of the risks is the production of acrylamide, a potentially harmful compound that forms when starchy foods (like potatoes) are cooked at high temperatures. To reduce the risk of acrylamide formation, avoid overcooking your potatoes and soak them in water for 30 minutes before cooking. Plus, choosing healthier cooking oils, such as olive oil, can help minimize the formation of harmful compounds.
- **The Risk of Accidental Burns.** As with any cooking appliance that generates heat, there is a risk of accidental burns. The Ninja Dual Zone Air Fryer can become hot during operation, so it's easy to come into contact with the hot surfaces and burn yourself. Therefore, be careful and always use oven mitts or heat-resistant gloves when handling your Ninja Dual Zone Air Fryer.

Tips and Tricks for the Ninja Dual Zone Air Fryer

- **Preparation is half the battle.** This could involve proper seasoning or simply cutting the food into the desired size and shape. Pat food items dry before cooking them to reduce excess moisture, which can affect the crispiness. Precook or par-cook some ingredients. For instance, you can precook chicken wings in the microwave to reduce the air frying time and help prevent dryness.
- **Use oil wisely.** While the Ninja Dual Zone Air Fryer is designed to cook with less oil, a light spray or brush of oil on your ingredients can enhance the crispiness and flavour. Use high smoke point oils like canola, olive, coconut, or grapeseed oil.
- **Check, check, check.** It's essential to check your food regularly during the cooking process to avoid overcooking and undercooking. The removable components, such as baskets and drawers, make this easy and manageable.
- **Marinating like a pro.** Marinating can elevate the flavours of your air-fried foods. Marinating is a whole new level of air frying, whether it's meat, veggies, or tofu. I encourage you to experiment with different marinades and explore new flavour combinations.
- **Spice it up!** Elevate your cooking experience with the Ninja Foodi by using a variety of herbs. spices, and seasoning blends. From classic aromatics such as oregano and garlic to more exotic options like smoked paprika and coriander, the possibilities are endless.
- **Accessories.** Experiment with accessories like baking pans, racks, silicone cases, and skewers for more cooking options. Check the user manual for recommended accessories and usage. To prevent food from sticking to the basket, you can use baking paper or air fryer-specific liners. Just make sure they are heat-resistant and safe for use in your Ninja Dual Zone Air Fryer.
- **Shake, shake, shake!** Most of the air fryer recipes require you to shake or flip the ingredients during the cooking process to promote even browning. Keep in mind that proper spacing and flipping allow the hot air to circulate the food; so do not overload the drawers.
- **Have fun!** Remember, the key to success in the kitchen is experimentation and having fun! Cooking and air frying specifically might take some trial and error to get your favorite meals just right. Don't limit yourself to traditional fried foods. Try making homemade snacks,

reheating leftovers, or even baking cakes in your Ninja Dual Zone Air Fryer. So go ahead, have fun, and enjoy the endless possibilities that the Ninja Dual Zone Air Fryer offers.

Frequently Asked Questions

1. What is the wattage of the Ninja Dual Zone Air Fryer?

It may vary depending on the model, but it typically ranges from 1400 watts to 1800 watts.

2. What is the temperature range of the Ninja Dual Zone Air Fryer?

The temperature range typically varies from model to model, but it can generally go from 105°F (40°C) to 450°F (232°C).

3. How do I adjust cooking times and temperatures for my recipes?

These parameters may need to be adjusted based on the food you're cooking. Refer to the product manual for guidance on adjusting settings.

4. What can I cook in the Ninja Dual Zone Air Fryer?

You can cook a wide variety of foods in the Ninja Dual Zone Air Fryer, including meats, vegetables, seafood, baked goods, and even dehydrated fruits.

5. What is the capacity of the Ninja Dual Zone Air Fryer?

It may vary depending on the model, but it typically ranges from 7.6 to 9.5 litres.

6. What temperature should different foods be cooked at?

When it comes to air frying, cooking food at proper temperatures is essential to the safety of your meals. Below you can find a food temperature guide for common meats.

- Chicken, turkey, duck 74 °C
- Beef, lamb, veal (rare) 52 °C
- Beef, lamb, veal (medium) 60 °C
- Beef, lamb, veal (well done) 71 °C
- Pork roasts, steaks & chops (medium) 63 °C
- Pork roasts, steaks & chops (well done) 71 °C
- Fish 60 °C
- Casseroles 74 °C
- Egg dishes 71 °C

7. Can I cook frozen foods without thawing in the air fryer?

Absolutely! You can cook frozen foods directly in the air fryer without thawing. It may take a little longer than fresh items, so adjust the cooking time accordingly.

8. Can I use the Ninja Dual Zone Air Fryer for baking or grilling?

Absolutely! My recipe collection contains great recipes for homemade bread, cookies, and pastries. For baking, use it similarly to an oven. Preheat the air fryer to the desired temperature for baking. Place a baking dish into the air fryer basket, making sure it fits comfortably inside; adjust the time and temperature, as needed. Monitor the baking process and make sure to check for doneness.

When it comes to grilling, place your food on the grill grate. Cook the food for the recommended time, and if necessary, flip or rotate the items to ensure even cooking. Keep in mind that the results won't be the same as outdoor grilling, but it can provide a grilled texture and flavour. Lovely!

9. What makes the Ninja Dual Zone Air Fryer different from other air fryers?

The Ninja Dual Zone Air Fryer stands out from the crowd for several reasons. First, it features two independent cooking zones, allowing you to cook two separate dishes simultaneously. This dual-zone feature not only saves time but also ensures that the flavours and aromas of different foods don't mix.

10. Can I use the Ninja Dual Zone Air Fryer for reheating leftovers?

To reduce food waste, use your air fryer for reheating leftovers. Your Ninja Dual Zone Air Fryer will bring back the texture and freshness to a wide range of dishes.

To sum up, the Ninja Dual Zone Air Fryer shifted my cooking routine. With its innovative design, dual cooking zones, and versatility, it become an indispensable thing in our home. Whether I am frying chips or baking a cake, this Ninja Dual Zone Air Fryer gives exceptional results every time. Now, I invite you to unleash your inner chef and discover the incredible potential of the Ninja Dual Zone Air Fryer! Happy cooking! Bon appétit!

CHAPTER 1 : BREAKFAST

Hash Brown Quiche Cups

Prep time: 10 minutes / Cook time: 30 minutes / Serves 8

Ingredients
- 4 large eggs
- Sea salt and ground black pepper, to taste
- 200g parsnip, trimmed and grated
- 50g butter, melted
- 100g pancetta, cubed
- 1 tbsp minced fresh chives
- 400g waxy potato (such as Charlotte)

Instructions
1. In a mixing bowl, whisk the eggs until pale and frothy.
2. Boil the potatoes for 15 minutes; drain. Peel the potatoes and coarsely grate them into a bowl.
3. Add the potatoes, along with the other ingredients, to the beaten eggs. Mix to combine well and divide the mixture between 8 lightly greased muffin cases.
4. Lower the muffin cases into the prepared drawers.
5. Select zone 1 and pair it with "BAKE" at 180°C for 15 minutes. Select "MATCH" followed by the "START/STOP" button.
6. Bon appétit!

Per Serving:
Calories: 188g / Fat: 12.6g / Carbs: 13.3g / Fibre: 2.2g / Protein: 6.1g

Mini Pizza Tarlets

Prep time: 10 minutes / Cook time: 13 minutes / Serves 8

Ingredients
- 350g filo pastry
- 100ml tomato sauce
- 1 tsp dried oregano
- 1 tsp dried basil
- 150g button mushrooms, chopped
- 200g pancetta, chopped
- 200g mozzarella cheese, crumbled
- 8 Kalamata olives, pitted and halved

Instructions
1. Start by preheating your Ninja Dual Zone Air Fryer to 180°C for 5 minutes. Brush 8 muffin cases with cooking spray.
2. Completely thaw phyllo dough according to package directions. Pile up the filo pastry on a flat surface. Now, cut it into 8 squares and press them into the muffin cases.
3. Divide the remaining Ingredients between the prepared muffin cases. Place the muffin cases in both drawers.
4. Select zone 1 and pair it with "BAKE" at 180°C for 13 minutes or until golden. Select "MATCH" followed by the "START/STOP" button.
5. Serve warm and enjoy!

Per Serving:
Calories: 364g / Fat: 24g / Carbs: 24.9g / Fibre: 2.1g / Protein: 6.1g

Baked Almond & Banana Porridge

Prep time: 5 minutes / Cook time: 20 minutes / Serves 6

Ingredients
- 1 tbsp coconut oil, melted
- 250g rolled oats
- 1 ½ cups almond milk
- 100ml honey
- 1/2 tsp ground cinnamon
- A pinch of grated nutmeg
- 2 large bananas, peeled and halved lengthwise

Instructions
1. Brush two baking tins with coconut oil. Thoroughly combine the oats, almond milk, 50ml of honey, and spices in a mixing bowl.
2. Now, spoon the mixture into the prepared baking tin and lower it into the zone 1 drawer.

3. In a separate baking tin, drizzle your bananas with the remaining 50ml of honey; place them in the zone 2 drawer.
4. Select zone 1 and pair it with "BAKE" at 180°C for 20 minutes. Select zone 2 and pair it with "AIR FRY" at 170°C for 15 minutes
5. Select "SYNC" followed by the "START/STOP" button. At the halfway point, stir the porridge and toss the peaches to ensure even browning.
6. Spoon warm porridge into serving bowls. Garnish your porridge with the caramelized banana. Bon appétit!

Per Serving:
Calories: 264g / Fat: 6.4g / Carbs: 44.4g / Fibre: 4.6g / Protein: 9.1g

Colourful Egg Cups

Prep time: 10 minutes / Cook time: 13 minutes / Serves 4

Ingredients
- 1 tbsp butter, melted
- 6 large whole eggs
- 100g sour cream
- 1 small courgette, chopped
- 1 small onion, chopped
- 1 large bell pepper, seeded and chopped
- 1/2 tsp dried oregano
- 1 tsp dried basil
- Sea salt and ground black pepper, to taste

Instructions
1. Grease 8 muffin cases with melted butter. Then, thoroughly combine the other ingredients.
2. Spoon the mixture into the prepared muffin cases. Place 4 muffin cases in each drawer.
3. Select zone 1 and pair it with "BAKE" at 180°C for 13 minutes. Select "MATCH" followed by the "START/STOP" button.
4. Bon appétit!

Per Serving:
Calories: 193g / Fat: 12.8g / Carbs: 7.7g / Fibre: 1.5g / Protein: 11.3g

Granola Raisin Bars

Prep time: 5 minutes / Cook time: 20 minutes / Serves 8

Ingredients
- 50g multi-grain hoop cereal
- 50g rye flakes
- 50g oats
- 50ml applesauce, unsweetened
- 100g agave syrup
- 50g coconut oil, room temperature
- 50g raw pepitas
- 50g almonds, slivered
- 1 tsp vanilla essence
- 1 tsp ground cinnamon
- 100g raisins

Instructions
1. Remove a crisper plate from your Ninja Dual Zone Air Fryer.
2. In a mixing bowl, thoroughly combine all the ingredients, except raisins. Line two roasting tins with baking parchment.
3. Tip the mixture into the prepared tin, pressing down lightly with a spatula. Add roasting tins to both drawers.
4. Select zone 1 and pair it with "BAKE" at 180°C for 20 minutes. Select "MATCH" to duplicate settings across both zones. Press the "START/STOP" button.
5. Bon appétit!

Per Serving:
Calories: 222g / Fat: 7.2g / Carbs: 36.7g / Fibre: 3.9g / Protein: 6.3g

Autumn Pumpkin Muffins

Prep time: 10 minutes / Cook time: 18 minutes / Serves 9

Ingredients
- 150g wholemeal flour
- 100g rolled oats, plus extra for sprinkling
- 1 ½ tsp bicarbonate of soda
- 1 tsp pumpkin spice mix
- 100g golden syrup

- 2 large eggs
- 200g pumpkin, canned
- 50ml coconut oil
- 100ml yoghurt

Instructions

1. Remove a crisper plate from your Ninja Dual Zone Air Fryer. Preheat the Ninja Dual Zone Air Fryer to 170°C for 5 minutes. Very lightly butter 9 muffin cases.
2. In a bowl, thoroughly combine all the dry ingredients. In a separate bowl, whisk the wet ingredients.
3. Slowly and gradually, add the liquid mixture to the dry ingredients. Spoon the batter into the prepared muffin cases. Place muffin cases in the cooking basket.
4. Select zone 1 and pair it with "BAKE" at 170°C for 18 minutes. Select "MATCH" followed by the "START/STOP" button.
5. Let your muffins sit on a cooling rack for about 10 minutes before unmolding and serving. Bon appétit!

Per Serving:
Calories: 214g / Fat: 7.7g / Carbs: 31g / Fibre: 2.3g / Protein: 6.3g

Toasted Bread with Breakfast Sausages

Prep time: 5 minutes / Cook time: 15 minutes / Serves 5

Ingredients

- 1 loaf of crusty bread, sliced
- 30ml extra-virgin olive oil
- Sea salt and ground black pepper, to taste
- 1 tsp dried oregano
- 400g breakfast sausages

Instructions

1. Toss the bread slices with olive oil, salt, black pepper, and oregano.
2. Place the bread slices in the zone 1 drawer and the breakfast sausages in the zone 2 drawer.
3. Select zone 1 and pair it with "BAKE" at 180°C for 5 minutes. Select zone 2 and pair it

with "AIR FRY" at 190°C for 15 minutes.
4. Select "SYNC" followed by the "START/STOP" button. When zone 2 time reaches 7 minutes, turn the breakfast sausages over and reinsert the drawer to continue cooking.
5. Serve warm toasted bread with breakfast sausages and enjoy!

Per Serving:
Calories: 534g / Fat: 20.7g / Carbs: 60.6g / Fibre: 5g / Protein: 25.5g

Croissant French Toast

Prep time: 10 minutes / Cook time: 15 minutes / Serves 4

Ingredients

- 2 large eggs
- 4 tbsp double cream
- 4 tbsp golden caster sugar
- 1 tsp cinnamon powder
- 1/2 tsp ground cloves
- 2 tbsp coconut oil, room temperature
- 4 medium croissants, halved lengthwise

Instructions

1. Line the base of the coking basket with baking paper.
2. In a mixing bowl, whisk the eggs, cream, sugar, cinnamon, cloves, and coconut oil.
3. Now, dip the croissant halves in the custard mixture until they are well coated on all sides. Divide them between drawers.
4. Select zone 1 and pair it with "AIR FRYER" at 180°C for 15 minutes. Select "MATCH" followed by the "START/STOP" button.
5. Bon appétit!

Per Serving:
Calories: 392g / Fat: 24g / Carbs: 36g / Fibre: 1.8g / Protein: 8.8g

Aromatic Banana Fritters

Prep time: 10 minutes / Cook time: 10 minutes / Serves 6

Ingredients

- 4 ripe bananas, peeled and cut into quarters
- 2 tbsp coconut shreds

- Batter:
- 80g plain flour
- 70g oat flour
- 1/2 tsp baking powder
- 1 tsp cinnamon powder
- 1/4 tsp ground cloves
- 2 tbsp golden syrup
- 1 tbsp coconut oil

Instructions

1. Line two baking tins with baking parchment.
2. In a mixing bowl, thoroughly combine all the Ingredients for the batter.
3. Dip the banana pieces in the batter and arrange them in both drawers.
4. Select zone 1 and pair it with "BAKE" at 180°C for 10 minutes. Select "MATCH" to duplicate settings across both zones. Press the "START/STOP" button.
5. To serve, garnish with coconut shreds and enjoy!

Per Serving:
Calories: 208g / Fat: 3.7g / Carbs: 41.6g / Fibre: 3.4g / Protein: 4.4g

Spicy Bacon Omelette

Prep time: 10 minutes / Cook time: 13 minutes / Serves 4

Ingredients

- 1 tbsp butter, melted
- 7 whole eggs
- 100g bacon lardons
- 100g cream cheese
- 1 small chilli pepper, seeded and chopped
- 1 large bell pepper, seeded and chopped
- Sea salt and ground black pepper, to taste

Instructions

1. Grease 8 muffin cases with melted butter. Then, thoroughly combine the other ingredients.
2. Spoon the mixture into the prepared muffin cases. Place 4 muffin cases in each drawer.
3. Select zone 1 and pair it with "BAKE" at 180°C for 13 minutes. Select "MATCH" followed by the "START/STOP" button.
4. Bon appétit!

Per Serving:
Calories: 340g / Fat: 28.7g / Carbs: 5.8g / Fibre: 1g / Protein: 15.1g

The Best Sticky Bun Ever

Prep time: 10 minutes / Cook time: 13 minutes / Serves 6

Ingredients

- 320g ready-rolled puff pastry
- 2 tbsp ground cinnamon
- 4 tbsp caster sugar
- 1 medium egg, beaten
- 60g icing sugar

Instructions

1. Line two baking trays with baking parchment. Unravel the pastry on a lightly floured work surface.
2. Mix the cinnamon and sugar in a bowl.
3. Sprinkle the cinnamon mixture all over the top of your pastry. Brush a little of the beaten egg over the pastry border.
4. Roll the pastry up to create a log; slice it into 12 rolls. Lower the rolls onto the prepared baking trays.
5. Brush them with the remaining beaten egg.
6. Select zone 1 and pair it with "BAKE" at 180°C for 13 minutes or until golden. Select "MATCH" followed by the "START/STOP" button.
7. Meanwhile, mix the icing sugar with 1 tablespoon of water. Drizzle your icing over the rolls and enjoy!

Per Serving:
Calories: 383g / Fat: 21.2g / Carbs: 44.5g / Fibre: 2.1g / Protein: 5g

Winter Frittata with Bacon

Prep time: 10 minutes / Cook time: 15 minutes / Serves 4

Ingredients

- 7 large eggs, beaten
- 1 small leek, sliced
- 150g bacon lardons
- A large handful of baby spinach, roughly chopped
- 2 tbsp fresh cilantro, chopped
- 1 tsp cayenne pepper

- Sea salt and ground black pepper, to taste

Instructions

1. Remove a crisper plate from your Ninja Dual Zone Air Fryer. Grease two baking trays with cooking oil.
2. In a mixing bowl, thoroughly combine all the ingredients. Spoon the mixture into the baking trays.
3. Lower them into the drawers.
4. Select zone 1 and pair it with "BAKE" at 180°C for 15 minutes. Select "MATCH" followed by the "START/STOP" button.
5. Cut each frittata into wedges and serve immediately. Bon appétit!

Per Serving:
Calories: 317g / Fat: 23.5g / Carbs: 8.5g / Fibre: 2.6g / Protein: 18.7g

Flapjacks with Golden Raisins

Prep time: 10 minutes / Cook time: 18 minutes / Serves 5

Ingredients

- 1 tbsp coconut oil
- 300g old-fashioned oats
- 50ml applesauce, unsweetened
- 150g golden syrup
- 100g butter, melted
- 1/2 tsp ground cloves
- 1/2 tsp cinnamon powder
- A pinch of sea salt
- 60g golden raisins

Instructions

1. Begin by preheating your Ninja Dual Zone Air Fryer to 180°C. Now, brush silicone muffin cases with coconut oil.
2. In your processor, mix the rolled oats, applesauce, golden syrup, butter, and spices; fold in golden raisins and stir until everything is well combined.
3. Spoon the batter into the prepared muffin cases and lower them into both drawers.
4. Select zone 1 and pair it with "AIR FRY" at 180°C for 18 minutes. Select zone 2 and pair it with "AIR FRY" at 200°C for 12 minutes.
5. Select "SYNC" followed by the "START/STOP" button.
6. Transfer your flapjacks to a cooling rack for about 10 minutes before unmolding.
7. Bon appétit!

Per Serving:
Calories: 525g / Fat: 23.2g / Carbs: 73.1g / Fibre: 7g / Protein: 10.7g

Mixed Berry Muffins

Prep time: 5 minutes / Cook time: 15 minutes / Serves 12

Ingredients

- 2 large eggs, beaten
- 20ml coconut oil
- 130ml natural yoghurt
- 2 extra-large ripe bananas, mashed
- 4 tbsp golden syrup
- 150g whole meal flour
- 100g rolled oats
- 1 ½ tsp baking powder
- 1 tsp bicarbonate of soda
- 1 tsp cinnamon
- A pinch of sea salt
- 50g cherries, pitted
- 100g blackberries

Instructions

1. Preheat your Ninja Dual Zone Air Fryer to 170°C for 5 minutes. Grease the inside of 12 muffin cases with cooking oil.
2. In a jug, thoroughly combine all the liquid ingredients. Tip the remaining ingredients, except the berries, into a separate mixing bowl; mix until everything is well combined.
3. Slowly and gradually, add the dry Ingredients to the liquid ingredients; fold in the berries and gently stir to combine.
4. Scrape the batter into the prepared muffin cases. Divide the muffin cases between drawers.
5. Select zone 1 and pair it with "BAKE" at 170°C for 15 minutes. Select "MATCH" followed by the "START/STOP" button.

6. Transfer your muffins to a wire rack and leave to cool.
7. Bon appétit!

Per Serving:
Calories: 155g / Fat: 3.5g / Carbs: 27.2g / Fibre: 3.5g / Protein: 5.7g

Bacon & Egg Bap

Prep time: 5 minutes / Cook time: 18 minutes / Serves 4

Ingredients
- 4 small rashers smoked bacon
- 4 eggs
- Sea salt and red pepper, to taste
- 1 tsp sunflower oil
- 300g can red kidney beans
- 4 large soft white baps

Instructions
1. Add smoked bacon to the zone 1 drawer.
2. Brush 4 muffin cases with sunflower oil and crack an egg into each of them; season with salt and pepper and add them to the zone 2 drawer.
3. Select zone 1 and pair it with "AIR FRY" at 200°C for 10 minutes. Select zone 2 and pair it with "AIR FRY" at 180°C for 13 minutes
4. Select "SYNC" followed by the "START/STOP" button.
5. Meanwhile, heat the beans in a saucepan.
6. Split the baps so they are still hinged at one edge. Add the bacon and eggs to your baps.
7. Use "REHEAT" mode to toast your baps at 160°C for 5 minutes. Serve warm baps with small pots of beans on the side.
8. Bon appétit!

Per Serving:
Calories: 285g / Fat: 16.5g / Carbs: 19.8g / Fibre: 2.5g / Protein: 12.4g

Breakfast Pie with Bacon

Prep time: 10 minutes / Cook time: 20 minutes / Serves 8

Ingredients
- 8 (about 350g) sheets of filo pastry
- 100ml tomato sauce
- 4 small eggs
- 4 spring onions, sliced
- 150g bacon, chopped
- 100g cheddar cheese, shredded

Instructions
1. Start by preheating your Ninja Dual Zone Air Fryer to 180°C for 5 minutes. Line two tart tins with baking paper.
2. Completely thaw phyllo dough according to package directions. Unfold the pastry and press 4 sheets of your filo pastry into each tart tin; make sure to leave a little pastry hanging over the edges.
3. Mix tomato sauce, eggs, and spring onions in a bowl. Divide the bacon between tart tins and lower them into both drawers.
4. Select zone 1 and pair it with "BAKE" at 180°C for 20 minutes or until golden. Select "MATCH" followed by the "START/STOP" button.
5. After 10 minutes, top each pie with cheese and reinsert the drawers to resume cooking. Devour!

Per Serving:
Calories: 382g / Fat: 27g / Carbs: 24.4g / Fibre: 1.6g / Protein: 10.4g

Italian-Style Mini Frittata

Prep time: 10 minutes / Cook time: 15 minutes / Serves 8

Ingredients
- 6 large eggs, beaten
- 4 tbsp plain milk
- 100g cheddar cheese, grated
- 1 large tomato, diced
- 1 tsp Italian spice mix
- 50g parmesan cheese, preferably freshly grated
- Sea salt and ground black pepper, to taste

Instructions
1. Remove a crisper plate from your Ninja Dual Zone Air Fryer. Grease 8 silicone muffin cases with nonstick cooking oil.
2. In a mixing bowl, thoroughly combine all the ingredients, except for parmesan cheese. Spoon

the mixture into the prepared muffin cases.

3. Lower the muffin cases into the drawers.
4. Select zone 1 and pair it with "BAKE" at 180°C for 15 minutes. Select "MATCH" followed by the "START/STOP" button.
5. At the halfway point, top mini frittatas with parmesan cheese and reinsert the drawers to resume cooking.
6. Bon appétit!

Per Serving:

Calories: 382g / Fat: 27g / Carbs: 24.4g / Fibre: 1.6g / Protein: 10.4g

Superfood Quinoa Porridge

Prep time: 10 minutes / Cook time: 15 minutes / Serves 4

Ingredients

* 2 tsp coconut oil, melted
* 300g quinoa, soaked overnight and rinsed
* 2 large bananas, peeled and mashed
* 1 litre milk
* 2 tbsp chia seeds
* 2 tbsp hemp seeds
* 4 tbsp maple syrup
* 1 vanilla bean, split
* 1 cinnamon stick
* 100g prunes, pitted and chopped

Instructions

1. Brush the inside of two baking trays with coconut oil.
2. Mix the quinoa with the other Ingredients and spoon the mixture into the baking trays. Add the baking trays to the drawers.
3. Select zone 1 and pair it with "BAKE" at 180°C for 15 minutes. Select "MATCH" to duplicate settings across both zones. Press the "START/STOP" button.
4. Spoon your porridge into serving bowls and serve with some extra fruits, if desired.
5. Bon appétit!

Per Serving:

Calories: 382g / Fat: 27g / Carbs: 24.4g / Fibre: 1.6g / Protein: 10.4g

Cornbread Muffins

Prep time: 10 minutes / Cook time: 25 minutes / Serves 6

Ingredients

* 50g butter, melted
* 100g sweetcorn kernels, frozen and thawed
* 2 small eggs
* 50ml milk
* 140ml pot buttermilk
* 80g plain flour
* 80g cornmeal
* 1 tsp baking powder
* 100g Parmesan cheese, grated

Instructions

1. Remove a crisper plate from your Ninja Foodi. Lightly spray muffin cases with cooking oil.
2. In a mixing bowl, thoroughly combine all the ingredients. Spoon the batter into the prepared muffin cases.
3. Add muffin cases to both drawers.
4. Select zone 1 and pair it with "BAKE" at 180°C for 25 minutes, until golden brown. Select "MATCH" to duplicate settings across both zones. Press the "START/STOP" button.
5. Bon appétit!

Per Serving:

Calories: 286g / Fat: 14g / Carbs: 29.1g / Fibre: 1.5g / Protein: 10.5g

Cinnamon Banana Bread Muffins

Prep time: 10 minutes / Cook time: 18 minutes / Serves 9

Ingredients

* 150g whole meal flour
* 100g rolled oats, plus extra for sprinkling
* 1/2 tsp baking powder
* 1 tsp bicarbonate of soda
* 1 tsp ground cinnamon
* A pinch of sea salt
* 2 large eggs
* 100ml almond milk
* 2 large very ripe bananas, mashed

- 100g golden syrup
- 50ml coconut oil

Instructions

1. Remove a crisper plate from your Ninja Dual Zone Air Fryer. Preheat the Ninja Dual Zone Air Fryer to 170°C for 5 minutes. Grease 9 muffin cases with cooking oil.
2. In a mixing bowl, thoroughly combine all the dry ingredients.
3. Slowly and gradually, add the wet Ingredients to the flour mixture; mix again to combine. Spoon the batter into the prepared muffin cases. Place muffin cases in both drawers.
4. Select zone 1 and pair it with "BAKE" at 170°C for 18 minutes. Select "MATCH" followed by the "START/STOP" button.
5. Bake until a toothpick inserted into the centre comes out dry and clean. Enjoy!

Per Serving:
Calories: 226g / Fat: 7.8g / Carbs: 36.3g / Fibre: 3.8g / Protein: 4.6g

Avocado Toast with Beans

Prep time: 5 minutes / Cook time: 5 minutes / Serves 5

Ingredients

- 1 loaf of crusty bread, sliced
- 20ml extra-virgin olive oil
- Sea salt and ground black pepper, to taste
- 1 tsp garlic granules
- 2 large avocados, pitted, cored, and sliced
- 1 tbsp fresh lemon juice
- 2 tbsp sesame seeds, toasted
- 200g canned pinto beans

Instructions

1. Toss the bread slices with olive oil, salt, black pepper, and garlic granules.
2. Place the bread slices in the cooking basket.
3. Select zone 1 and pair it with "AIR FRY" at 180°C for 5 minutes. Select "MATCH" to duplicate settings across both zones. Press the "START/STOP" button.
4. Toss avocado slices with lemon juice and

sesame seeds.
5. Top warm toasted bread with avocado and pinto beans. Serve immediately and enjoy!

Per Serving:
Calories: 477g / Fat: 21.1g / Carbs: 60g / Fibre: 11.8g / Protein: 1.1g

Omelette with Spinach and Pancetta

Prep time: 10 minutes / Cook time: 13 minutes / Serves 4

Ingredients

- 5 large eggs, beaten
- 1 tbsp olive oil
- 2 tbsp chives, chopped
- 1 tsp paprika
- Sea salt and ground black pepper, to taste
- 150g pancetta slices, thick cut
- A large handful of baby spinach, roughly chopped

Instructions

1. Grease a baking tray with cooking oil.
2. In a mixing bowl, thoroughly combine the eggs, olive oil, chives, paprika, salt, and black pepper. Spoon the mixture into the prepared baking tray.
3. Lower the baking tray into the zone 1 drawer. Add pancetta slices to the zone 2 drawer (with a crisper plate).
4. Select zone 1 and pair it with "AIR FRY" at 180°C for 13 minutes. Select zone 2 and pair it with "AIR FRY" at 200°C for 12 minutes.
5. Select "SYNC" followed by the "START/ STOP" button. At the halfway point, turn pancetta slices over with silicone-tipped tongs to promote even cooking.
6. Cut the pancetta into bite-sized pieces.
7. Cut your omelette into four wedges. Scatter baby spinach and pancetta over the top of the omelette and fold gently in half with a wide spatula.
8. Slide onto a plate and serve immediately. Devour!

Per Serving:
Calories: 224g / Fat: 18.5g / Carbs: 3.7g / Fibre: 1.5g / Protein: 11g

CHAPTER 2 : BEANS & GRAINS

Italian-Style Macaroni Bake

Prep time: 10 minutes / Cook time: 25 minutes / Serves 5

Ingredients

- 300g macaroni
- 500g Italian sausage, meat squeezed from the skins
- 200ml vegetable broth
- 1 tsp Italian spice mix
- Sea salt and ground black pepper, to taste
- 2 medium ripe tomatoes, chopped
- 100g gruyere cheese, grated

Instructions

1. Cook your macaroni following pack Instructions; drain and reserve.
2. Add all the ingredients, except the cheese, to a large bowl and stir until everything is well combined.
3. Spoon the mixture into two lightly greased baking trays. Add the baking trays to the drawers (without crisper plates).
4. Select zone 1 and pair it with "BAKE" at 180°C for 25 minutes. Select "MATCH" followed by the "START/STOP" button.
5. At the halfway point, gently stir the Ingredients using a wooden spoon. Top with gruyere cheese and reinsert drawers to resume cooking.
6. Bon appétit!

Per Serving:
Calories: 572g / Fat: 28.1g / Carbs: 52.8g / Fibre: 2.9g / Protein: 25.8g

Cheesy Polenta Muffins

Prep time: 10 minutes / Cook time: 25 minutes / Serves 6

Ingredients

- 50ml olive oil
- 2 small eggs
- 100ml milk
- 50ml sparkling water
- 100g plain flour
- 100g cornmeal
- 1 tsp baking powder
- 60g gruyere cheese, grated

Instructions

1. Remove a crisper plate from your Ninja Foodi. Lightly spray muffin cases with cooking oil.
2. In a mixing bowl, thoroughly combine all the ingredients. Spoon the batter into the prepared muffin cases.
3. Add muffin cases to both drawers.
4. Select zone 1 and pair it with "BAKE" at 180°C for 25 minutes, until golden brown. Select "MATCH" to duplicate settings across both zones. Press the "START/STOP" button.
5. Bon appétit!

Per Serving:
Calories: 269g / Fat: 13.7g / Carbs: 26.8g / Fibre: 1.2g / Protein: 8g

Quinoa Green Bean Pilaf

Prep time: 10 minutes / Cook time: 18 minutes / Serves 5

Ingredients

- 2 tsp olive oil, melted
- 300g quinoa, soaked overnight and rinsed
- 1 litre vegetable broth
- 1 shallot, minced
- 2 garlic cloves, minced
- 1 bell pepper, deseeded and sliced
- 300g green beans

Instructions

1. Brush the inside of two baking trays with olive oil.
2. Mix the quinoa with the other Ingredients and spoon the mixture into the baking trays. Add the baking trays to the drawers.
3. Select zone 1 and pair it with "BAKE" at

180°C for 18 minutes. Select "MATCH" to duplicate settings across both zones. Press the "START/STOP" button.

4. Spoon your pilaf into serving bowls and serve immediately. Enjoy!

Per Serving:

Calories: 309g / Fat: 6.9g / Carbs: 48.5g / Fibre: 6.7g / Protein: 14.4g

Maple Granola Crunch Porridge

Prep time: 5 minutes / Cook time: 12 minutes / Serves 9

Ingredients

- 100g rye flakes
- 250g rolled oats
- 100g almond butter
- 100g almonds, slivered
- 100g maple syrup
- 1/2 tsp ground cloves
- 1/2 tsp ground cinnamon
- A pinch of coarse sea salt
- 50g hemp seeds
- 50g sunflower seeds
- 50g pumpkin seeds

Instructions

1. In a mixing bowl, thoroughly combine all the ingredients. Now, press the mixture into two parchment-lined roasting tins; press down slightly using a wide spatula.
2. Place the roasting tins in both drawers.
3. Select zone 1 and pair it with "BAKE" at 180°C for 12 minutes. Select "MATCH" followed by the "START/STOP" button.
4. When zone 1 time reaches 6 minutes, stir the mixture and reinsert the drawer to continue cooking.
5. Bon appétit!

Per Serving:

Calories: 421g / Fat: 25.6g / Carbs: 38.7g / Fibre: 6.9g / Protein: 12.9g

Garbanzo Bean Patties

Prep time: 10 minutes / Cook time: 20 minutes / Serves 6

Ingredients

- 1 (400g) can garbanzo beans, rinsed and drained
- 300g quinoa, soaked overnight and rinsed
- 1 medium onion, peeled
- 2 garlic cloves
- 100g tortilla chips, crushed
- 1 tsp smoked paprika
- 1/2 tsp coriander seeds, ground
- 1/2 tsp cumin seeds
- Sea salt and ground black pepper, to taste

Instructions

1. Insert the crisper plates in both drawers and spray them with cooking oil.
2. In your blender, process all the Ingredients until a thick and uniform batter is formed. Shape the mixture into equal patties.
3. Now, spray the patties with nonstick cooking oil and then, place them on the crisper plates.
4. Select zone 1 and pair it with "AIR FRY" at 190°C for 20 minutes. Select "MATCH" to duplicate settings across both zones. Press the "START/STOP" button.
5. When zone 1 time reaches 10 minutes, turn the patties over and spray them with cooking oil on the other side; then, reinsert the drawers to continue cooking.
6. Serve warm patties on burger buns and enjoy!

Per Serving:

Calories: 339g / Fat: 8.1g / Carbs: 55.9g / Fibre: 7.6g / Protein: 11.6g

Oatmeal Nutty Muffins

Prep time: 10 minutes / Cook time: 20 minutes / Serves 6

Ingredients

- 1 tbsp coconut oil
- 1 medium egg, beaten
- 200ml almond milk
- 250g old-fashioned oats
- 1 tbsp ground flaxseed meal
- 1 tsp baking powder
- 50ml clear honey

- 1 tsp ground cinnamon
- A pinch of grated nutmeg
- A pinch of sea salt

Instructions

1. Brush the inside of 6 muffin cases with coconut oil.
2. Thoroughly combine all the Ingredients and spoon the mixture into the prepared muffin cases. Add the muffin cases to the drawers.
3. Select zone 1 and pair it with "BAKE" at 190°C for 20 minutes. Select "MATCH" to duplicate settings across both zones. Press the "START/STOP" button.
4. Let the muffins stand on a cooling rack for about 10 minutes before unmolding and serving.
5. Bon appétit!

Per Serving:
Calories: 244g / Fat: 7.2g / Carbs: 36.9g / Fibre: 5.1g / Protein: 9.4g

Burritos with Roasted Peppers

Prep time: 10 minutes / Cook time: 15 minutes / Serves 4

Ingredients

- 4 medium peppers, deseeded and quartered
- Sea salt and ground black pepper, to taste
- 1/2 tsp paprika
- 1 tsp garlic granules
- 4 large tortillas
- 100g sweet corn kernels, frozen and thawed
- 100g canned black beans, drained and rinsed
- 50ml salsa
- 1 medium tomato, chopped
- 1 small onion, thinly sliced

Instructions

1. Insert a crisper plate in both drawers. Spray the plates with nonstick cooking oil.
2. Toss the peppers with salt, black pepper, paprika, and garlic granules.
3. Add peppers to the zone 1 drawer; add the tortilla wraps to the zone 2 drawer.
4. Select zone 1 and pair it with "AIR FRY" at

195°C for 10 minutes. Select zone 2 and pair it with "BAKE" at 180°C for 5 minutes
5. Select "SYNC" followed by the "START/STOP" button. At the halfway point, turn your food over to ensure even cooking.
6. To assemble your burritos: divide all the Ingredients between tortillas and wrap them up.
7. Add burritos to the drawers. Select zone 1 and pair it with "REHEAT" at 160°C for 5 minutes. Enjoy!

Per Serving:
Calories: 447g / Fat: 7.7g / Carbs: 82g / Fibre: 8.9g / Protein: 14.4g

Easy Bean Curry

Prep time: 10 minutes / Cook time: 24 minutes / Serves 4

Ingredients

- 2 tsp olive oil
- 1 shallot, chopped
- 2 medium peppers, deseeded and sliced
- 2 garlic cloves, finely chopped
- 1 bay leaf
- 1 tsp garam masala
- 1 tsp turmeric powder
- 400g red kidney beans, drained and rinsed
- 1 (400g) can tomatoes, chopped
- 100ml coconut milk
- 2 tbsp fresh cilantro leaves, chopped

Instructions

1. Heat 1 teaspoon of olive oil in a pan over medium-high heat. Sauté the shallot and peppers for about 3 minutes, until just tender.
2. Then, sauté the garlic and bay leaf for about 30 seconds, until fragrant.
3. Brush the inside of two baking tins with the remaining 1 teaspoon of olive oil. Add the sauteed mixture along with the spices, beans, and tomatoes to the baking tins; gently stir to combine and lower them into the drawers.
4. Select zone 1 and pair it with "AIR FRY" at 180°C for 20 minutes. Select "MATCH" to

duplicate settings across both zones. Press the "START/STOP" button.

5. When zone 1 time reaches 10 minutes, add the coconut milk and gently stir your curry; reinsert the drawers to continue cooking.
6. Spoon your curry into serving bowls and garnish with cilantro. Devour!

Per Serving:
Calories: 255g / Fat: 9.7g / Carbs: 34.7g / Fibre: 10g / Protein: 10.7g

Authentic Mexican Quesadilla

Prep time: 10 minutes / Cook time: 23 minutes / Serves 4

Ingredients
* 200g chorizo sausage, casing removed, sliced
* 200g pinto beans with onions, rinsed and drained
* 2 tsp olive oil
* 1 tsp paprika
* 1 tsp garlic granules
* Sea salt and ground black pepper, to taste
* Quesadillas:
* 8 small tortillas
* 100g cheddar cheese, grated
* 100g tub fresh tomato salsa

Instructions
1. Grease a baking tray with 1 tsp of olive oil; now, thoroughly combine the beans, and spices in the baking tray.
2. Add the baking tray to the zone 1 drawer and sausages to the zone 2 drawer (with a crisper plate inserted). Brush your sausages with the remaining 1 teaspoon of olive oil.
3. Select zone 1 and pair it with "BAKE" at 180°C for 15 minutes. Select zone 2 and pair it with "AIR FRY" at 200°C for 15 minutes
4. Select "SYNC" followed by the "START/STOP" button. At the halfway point, flip the sausages over to ensure even cooking.
5. Spread the refried beans and sausages onto 3 tortillas; scatter over the grated cheese. Add the salsa and top with the remaining tortillas.
6. Select "REHEAT" at 170°C for 8 minutes until your quesadillas are golden on the top. Serve warm and enjoy!

Per Serving:
Calories: 437g / Fat: 18.1g / Carbs: 50g / Fibre: 6.6g / Protein: 18.5g

Three Bean Chilli

Prep time: 10 minutes / Cook time: 20 minutes / Serves 6

Ingredients
* 200g cooked or canned pinto beans, drained and rinsed
* 300g cooked or canned red beans, drained and rinsed
* 300g cooked or canned black beans, drained and rinsed
* 1 thyme sprig, chopped
* 1 bay leaf
* 1 chilli pepper, chopped
* 1 tbsp vegetable oil
* 50ml tomato sauce
* 1 medium leek, chopped
* 2 garlic cloves, sliced
* 1 (460g) jar roasted red peppers, sliced
* 1 tbsp hot paprika
* 1 tbsp dried Mexican oregano
* Sea salt and ground black pepper, to taste
* 200ml chicken broth

Instructions
1. In a mixing bowl, thoroughly combine the beans with the other ingredients.
2. Transfer the bean mixture to two lightly greased baking trays. Add the baking trays to the cooking basket.
3. Select zone 1 and pair it with "BAKE" at 180°C for 20 minutes. Select "MATCH" followed by the "START/STOP" button.
4. Devour!

Per Serving:
Calories: 255g / Fat: 3.7g / Carbs: 43.1g / Fibre: 11.5g / Protein: 14.2g

Millet and Vegetable Bake

Prep time: 10 minutes / Cook time: 17 minutes / Serves 4

Ingredients

- 1 tbsp olive oil
- 150g millet grain
- 450ml vegetable stock
- 1 medium shallot, sliced
- 200g Brussel sprouts, rough outer leaves, trimmed and halved
- 1 medium head of broccoli, trimmed and cut into small florets
- 1 tsp dried basil
- 1 tsp dried oregano
- 1 tsp dried parsley flakes
- Sea salt and ground black pepper, to taste
- 100g cheddar cheese, grated

Instructions

1. Brush the inside of two oven-safe baking trays with olive oil.
2. Tip the millet into baking trays; add in the vegetables and spices, and stir to combine.
3. Add the baking tins to the drawers.
4. Select zone 1 and pair it with "BAKE" at 180°C for 17 minutes. Select "MATCH" to duplicate settings across both zones. Press the "START/STOP" button.
5. When zone 1 time reaches 8 minutes, scatter cheese over the top and reinsert the drawers to continue cooking.
6. Bon appétit!

Per Serving:
Calories: 383g / Fat: 14.2g / Carbs: 48.4g / Fibre: 10.4g / Protein: 19.8g

Healthy Pancakes

Prep time: 10 minutes / Cook time: 20 minutes / Serves 4

Ingredients

- 1 tbsp coconut oil, melted
- 2 small bananas, mashed
- 200g rolled oats
- 100g clear honey
- 50g peanut butter, melted
- A pinch of sea salt
- 1/4 tsp grated nutmeg
- 1/2 tsp cinnamon powder

Instructions

1. Grease two muffin tins with the melted coconut oil.
2. In your food processor, mix all the Ingredients until everything is well incorporated.
3. Spoon the batter into the prepared muffin tins. Lower one muffin tin into each drawer.
4. Select zone 1 and pair it with "AIR FRY" at 185°C for 20 minutes. Select "MATCH" followed by the "START/STOP" button.
5. Serve your pancakes with toppings of choice. Bon appétit!

Per Serving:
Calories: 420g / Fat: 13.3g / Carbs: 69g / Fibre: 7.9g / Protein: 12.1g

Mushroom Risotto with Beans

Prep time: 10 minutes / Cook time: 22 minutes / Serves 6

Ingredients

- 1 tbsp butter, room temperature
- 1 medium leek, chopped
- 2 garlic cloves, sliced
- 1 bay leaf
- 2 tbsp fresh chives, roughly chopped
- 350g risotto rice
- 600ml vegetable broth
- 100g cremini mushrooms, sliced
- 200g canned red kidney beans, drained and rinsed

Instructions

1. Remove a crisper plate from your Ninja Foodi. Lightly grease two baking tins and set them aside.
2. Melt the butter in a frying pan over medium-high heat; sauté the leek for about 3 minutes. Add the garlic and bay leaf; let it cook for 1 minute more, until fragrant. Divide the sauteed mixture between two baking tins.

3. Tip in the rice and the remaining ingredients. Add baking tins to the drawers.
4. Select zone 1 and pair it with "BAKE" at 180°C for 18 minutes. Select "MATCH" to duplicate settings across both zones. Press the "START/STOP" button.
5. At the halfway point, gently stir your risotto to promote even cooking; reinsert the drawers to resume cooking.
6. Bon appétit!

Per Serving:
Calories: 306g / Fat: 3.1g / Carbs: 58.6g / Fibre: 4.7g / Protein: 9.7g

Baked Oats with Walnuts & Plums

Prep time: 10 minutes / Cook time: 20 minutes / Serves 7

Ingredients
- 2 tsp coconut oil, melted
- 400g old-fashioned oats
- 200ml full-fat coconut milk
- 100g plums, pitted and sliced
- 100g walnut halves
- 1 tsp baking powder
- 1/2 cup honey
- A pinch of ground cinnamon
- 1 tsp vanilla bean paste
- A pinch of grated nutmeg

Instructions
1. Brush the inside of two baking tins with coconut oil.
2. Mix all the Ingredients in your blender or food processor. Now, spoon the mixture into the baking tins.
3. Select zone 1 and pair it with "BAKE" at 185°C for 20 minutes. Select "MATCH" to duplicate settings across both zones. Press the "START/STOP" button.
4. When zone 1 time reaches 10 minutes, turn the baking tins and reinsert the drawers to continue cooking.
5. Bon appétit!

Per Serving:
Calories: 476g / Fat: 21.4g / Carbs: 63.4g / Fibre: 7.9g / Protein: 12.7g

Twisted Fried Rice

Prep time: 10 minutes / Cook time: 20 minutes / Serves 4

Ingredients
- 2 tsp olive oil
- 300g rice, cooked and chilled
- 1 shallot, chopped
- 1 tsp ginger-garlic paste
- 2 tbsp soy sauce
- 1 medium carrot, trimmed and chopped
- 200g canned or cooked red kidney beans, drained and rinsed
- 200g cauliflower florets
- Sea salt and ground black pepper, to taste
- 1 large eggs, whisked

Instructions
1. Mix 1 teaspoon of olive oil and rice in a baking tray. Stir in the shallot, ginger-garlic paste, soy sauce, carrot, and beans. Lower the baking tray into the zone 1 drawer.
2. Toss cauliflower florets with the remaining 1 teaspoon of oil, salt, and black pepper; lower them into the zone 2 drawer (with a crisper plate).
3. Select zone 1 and pair it with "BAKE" at 180°C for 20 minutes. Select zone 2 and pair it with "ROAST" at 200°C for 8 minutes. Select "SYNC" followed by the "START/STOP" button.
4. When zone 1 time reaches 5 minutes, stir the egg into your rice and reinsert the drawer to continue cooking.
5. When zone 2 time reaches 4 minutes, shake the drawer to ensure even cooking; reinsert the drawer to continue cooking.
6. Add the cauliflower florets to fried rice and serve immediately. Devour!

Per Serving:
Calories: 226g / Fat: 5.4g / Carbs: 36.6g / Fibre: 4.5g / Protein: 7.9g

Spicy Double Bean Casserole

Prep time: 10 minutes / Cook time: 30 minutes / Serves 6

Ingredients

- 400g macaroni
- 200g canned or cooked red kidney beans, rinsed and drained
- 200g canned or cooked garbanzo beans, rinsed and drained
- 200ml chicken stock
- 200ml tomato sauce
- Sea salt and ground black pepper, to taste
- 1 large bell pepper, deseeded and sliced
- 2 celery sticks, finely chopped
- 1 onion, sliced
- 2 garlic cloves, chopped
- 150g Parmesan cheese, preferably freshly grated
- 50g breadcrumbs

Instructions

1. Cook your macaroni following pack Instructions; drain and reserve.
2. Thoroughly combine the beans, stock, tomato sauce, salt, black pepper, and vegetables in a large bowl; gently stir to combine.
3. Spoon the mixture into two lightly greased baking trays. Add the baking trays to the drawers (without crisper plates).
4. Select zone 1 and pair it with "BAKE" at 180°C for 30 minutes. Select "MATCH" followed by the "START/STOP" button.
5. At the halfway point, gently stir the Ingredients using a wooden spoon. Top with cheese and breadcrumbs; reinsert drawers to resume cooking.
6. Bon appétit!

Per Serving:
Calories: 496g / Fat: 9.6g / Carbs: 78.3g / Fibre: 7.5g / Protein: 24g

Easy Chicken Taquitos

Prep time: 10 minutes / Cook time: 26 minutes / Serves 6

Ingredients

- 400g chicken breast
- 1 tsp olive oil
- 1 tbsp taco seasoning mix
- Sea salt and ground black pepper, to taste
- 100g sweet corn kernels, frozen and thawed
- 300g canned red kidney beans, rinsed and drained
- 12 small corn tortillas
- 150g Mexican blend cheese, crumbled
- 100g tub fresh tomato salsa

Instructions

1. Toss the chicken with olive oil, taco seasoning mix, salt, and pepper. Lower the chicken into the cooking basket; air fry the chicken breasts at 190°C for 18 minutes, until thoroughly cooked.
2. Cut the chicken into strips; add the remaining Ingredients to the chicken and gently stir to combine.
3. Lightly grease a baking tray with cooking oil.
4. Divide the chicken/cheese filling between corn tortillas and roll them up tightly. Place your taquitos, seam side down, on the prepared baking tray.
5. Select "REHEAT" at 170°C for 8 minutes until your taquitos are golden on the top.
6. Serve immediately and enjoy!

Per Serving:
Calories: 416g / Fat: 17.2g / Carbs: 37.8g / Fibre: 7.6g / Protein: 27.3g

Bean & Mushroom Fritters

Prep time: 10 minutes / Cook time: 20 minutes / Serves 6

Ingredients

- 1 (400g) can red kidney beans, rinsed and drained
- 300g millet, soaked overnight and rinsed
- 100g mushrooms, chopped
- 1 medium onion, chopped
- 2 garlic cloves, minced
- 150g breadcrumbs

- 1 tsp smoked paprika
- 1/2 tsp cumin seeds
- Sea salt and ground black pepper, to taste

Instructions

1. Insert the crisper plates in both drawers and spray them with cooking oil.
2. Thoroughly combine all the Ingredients in a bowl. Shape the mixture into equal balls.
3. Now, spray the balls with cooking oil and lower them onto the crisper plates. Flatten them gently using a fork.
4. Select zone 1 and pair it with "AIR FRY" at 180°C for 20 minutes. Select "MATCH" to duplicate settings across both zones. Press the "START/STOP" button.
5. When zone 1 time reaches 10 minutes, turn the patties over and spray them with cooking oil on the other side; then, reinsert the drawers to continue cooking. Enjoy!

Per Serving:
Calories: 353g / Fat: 3.1g / Carbs: 65.9g / Fibre: 11.6g / Protein: 14.8g

Mexican-Style Black Bean Cakes

Prep time: 10 minutes / Cook time: 20 minutes / Serves 6

Ingredients

- 1 (400g) can black beans, rinsed, drained, and mashed
- 300g buckwheat, soaked overnight and rinsed
- 1 medium leek, chopped
- 2 garlic cloves, minced
- 100g bread crumbs
- 1 tsp English mustard
- 1 tsp smoked paprika
- 1/2 tsp cumin seeds
- Sea salt and ground black pepper, to taste

Instructions

1. Insert the crisper plates in both drawers and

spray them with cooking oil.
2. Thoroughly combine all the Ingredients in a bowl. Shape the mixture into equal balls.
3. Now, spray the balls with cooking oil and lower them onto the crisper plates.
4. Select zone 1 and pair it with "AIR FRY" at 180°C for 20 minutes. Select "MATCH" to duplicate settings across both zones. Press the "START/STOP" button.
5. Shake the basket halfway through the cooking time to promote even cooking.
6. Enjoy!

Per Serving:
Calories: 343g / Fat: 2.7g / Carbs: 68g / Fibre: 11.8g / Protein: 14.8g

Spicy Peppery Millet Porridge

Prep time: 10 minutes / Cook time: 20 minutes / Serves 6

Ingredients

- 2 tsp olive oil, melted
- 300g millet, soaked overnight and rinsed
- 800ml vegetable broth
- 2 garlic cloves, minced
- 1 bell pepper, deseeded and sliced
- 1 chilli pepper, deseeded and sliced

Instructions

1. Brush the inside of two baking trays with olive oil.
2. Mix the quinoa with the other Ingredients and spoon the mixture into the baking trays. Add the baking trays to the drawers.
3. Select zone 1 and pair it with "BAKE" at 180°C for 20 minutes. Select "MATCH" to duplicate settings across both zones. Press the "START/STOP" button.
4. Spoon your pilaf into serving bowls and serve immediately. Enjoy!

Per Serving:
Calories: 234g / Fat: 4.5g / Carbs: 39.1g / Fibre: 4.8g / Protein: 8.6g

Easy Polenta Ragout

Prep time: 10 minutes / Cook time: 20 minutes / Serves 5

Ingredients

- 500ml milk
- 250g instant polenta
- 50g butter
- 500g beef mince
- 1 shallot, finely sliced
- 2 garlic cloves, crushed
- Sea salt and ground black pepper, to taste
- 100g taleggio cheese, sliced

Instructions

1. Cook your polenta with milk according to the package Instructions; fold in the butter and whisk to combine well.
2. Spoon the polenta into two baking trays.
3. Mix the beef mince, shallot, garlic, salt, and black pepper. Spoon the beef mixture into the baking trays.
4. Select zone 1 and pair it with "BAKE" at 180°C for 20 minutes, until golden brown. Select "MATCH" to duplicate settings across both zones. Press the "START/STOP" button.
5. When zone 1 time reaches 10 minutes, top your polenta with cheese and reinsert the drawers to resume cooking.
6. Bon appétit!

Per Serving:

Calories: 580g / Fat: 30.3g / Carbs: 49.5g / Fibre: 4.5g / Protein: 30.2g

Authentic Lasagna

Prep time: 10 minutes / Cook time: 27 minutes / Serves 8

Ingredients

- Lasagna:
- 400g lasagna sheets
- 400g Italian sausage, meat squeezed from the skins
- 200ml vegetable broth
- 1 tsp dried oregano
- 1 tsp dried basil
- 1 tsp dried parsley flakes
- Sea salt and ground black pepper, to taste
- 400g can tomatoes
- 50g Parmesan cheese, grated
- Béchamel Sauce:
- 80g butter
- 80g plain flour
- 1.5l milk
- Sea salt and ground black pepper, to taste
- A pinch of grated nutmeg

Instructions

1. Cook lasagna sheets following pack Instructions; drain and reserve.
2. Mix the sausage, broth, spices, and tomatoes; stir until everything is well combined.
3. To make the béchamel sauce, melt the butter in a saucepan; then, cook the flour for 2 minutes, stirring continuously to avoid lumps.
4. Stir in the milk, a little at a time. Bring to a gentle simmer, whisking constantly. Season with salt, pepper, and nutmeg.
5. In two lightly greased baking trays, repeat the layers– lasagna sheets, béchamel, sausage sauce and parmesan cheese. Repeat until you run out of your ingredients.
6. Add the baking trays to the drawers (without crisper plates).
7. Select zone 1 and pair it with "BAKE" at 180°C for 25 minutes. Select "MATCH" followed by the "START/STOP" button.
8. Bon appétit!

Per Serving:

Calories: 605g / Fat: 32.5g / Carbs: 56.9g / Fibre: 5.5g / Protein: 23.9g

CHAPTER 3 : POULTRY

BBQ Duck Wings

Prep time: 5 minutes / Cook time: 25 minutes / Serves 4

Ingredients
- 1 kg duck wings, boneless
- 1 tbsp olive oil
- 1 tbsp maple syrup
- 1 tsp ginger-garlic paste
- 100ml BBQ sauce
- Sea salt and ground black pepper, to taste

Instructions
1. In a mixing bowl, toss the duck wings with the other ingredients. Add the wings to the cooking basket.
2. Select zone 1 and pair it with "AIR FRY" at 195°C for 25 minutes. Select "MATCH" to duplicate settings across both zones. Press the "START/STOP" button.
3. When zone 1 time reaches 15 minutes, turn the duck wings over and baste them with the remaining sauce. Reinsert the drawers to resume cooking.
4. Bon appétit!

Per Serving:
Calories: 265g / Fat: 4.5g / Carbs: 6.1g / Fibre: 0.6g / Protein: 51.1g

Peppercorn Chicken

Prep time: 10 minutes / Cook time: 25 minutes / Serves 6

Ingredients
- 1kg chicken drumettes, bone-in, skin-on
- 2 garlic cloves
- 1 tsp coarse sea salt
- 1 tbsp whole black peppercorns
- 1 bay leaf
- 1 tsp olive oil

Instructions
1. Pat the chicken drumettes dry using tea towels.
2. Crush the garlic and spices using a pestle and mortar. Rub the chicken with the oil and spice mix.
3. Place the prepared chicken drumettes in the cooking basket, skin-side down.
4. Select zone 1 and pair it with "AIR FRY" at 190°C for 25 minutes. Select "MATCH" followed by the "START/STOP" button.
5. When zone 1 time reaches 15 minutes, turn them over, and reinsert the drawer to continue cooking.
6. Bon appétit!

Per Serving:
Calories: 440g / Fat: 34.5g / Carbs: 0.5g / Fibre: 0g / Protein: 29.3g

Creamy Chicken Breasts

Prep time: 10 minutes / Cook time: 19 minutes / Serves 6

Ingredients
- 800g chicken breast fillets
- 1 tsp olive oil
- 1 tsp cayenne pepper
- Sea salt and ground black pepper, to taste
- 1 tbsp butter
- 2 cloves garlic, crushed
- 50ml chicken stock
- 50g cream

Instructions
1. Toss chicken breast fillets with olive oil, cayenne pepper, salt, and black pepper. Add the chicken fillets to baking tins and add them to both drawers.
2. Then, mix the remaining Ingredients until everything is well incorporated.
3. Select zone 1 and pair it with "BAKE" at 190°C for 19 minutes. Select "MATCH" followed by the "START/STOP" button.
4. When zone 1 time reaches 10 minutes, turn the chicken fillets over and top them with the sauce; reinsert the drawers to continue cooking.

5.Serve warm and enjoy!
Per Serving:
Calories: 284g / Fat: 16.9g / Carbs: 2.2g /
Fibre: 0.2g / Protein: 28.5g

Mexican-Style Chicken Meatloaf

Prep time: 10 minutes / Cook time: 20 minutes / Serves 8

Ingredients
* 1kg chicken breasts, chopped
* 1 garlic clove, minced
* 1 medium onion, chopped
* 1 jalapeno pepper, deseeded and minced
* 1 celery stalk, chopped
* 2 medium bell peppers, deseeded and halved
* 1 tbsp taco spice mix
* Sea salt and ground black pepper, to taste
* 1 medium eggs, beaten
* 50ml buttermilk
* 100g sharp cheese, grated

Instructions
1.Brush two loaf tins with nonstick cooking oil.
2.In a mixing bowl, thoroughly combine all the ingredients. Scrape the mixture into the prepared loaf tins.
3.Spray the top of your meatloaves with cooking oil. Add a loaf tin to each drawer.
4.Select zone 1 and pair it with "AIR FRY" at 180°C for 20 minutes. Select "MATCH" to duplicate settings across both zones. Press the "START/STOP" button.
5.Let your meatloaves sit for approximately 10 minutes before slicing and serving. Enjoy!
Per Serving:
Calories: 285g / Fat: 14.8g / Carbs: 5.5g /
Fibre: 1.1g / Protein: 29.6g

Easy Turkey Enchiladas

Prep time: 10 minutes / Cook time: 1 hour 3 minutes/ Serves 5

Ingredients
* 900g turkey, skinless and boneless, cut into bite-sized pieces
* Sea salt and ground black pepper, to taste
* 1 tsp olive oil
* 9 small tortillas
* 100g gruyere cheese, crumbled
* Enchilada Sauce:
* 1 tbsp olive oil
* 2 spring onions, chopped
* 1 garlic clove, crushed
* 100ml tomato sauce
* 100ml chicken bone broth
* 1 chilli pepper, minced

Instructions
1.Insert crisper plates in zone 1 and 2 drawers. Spray the crisper plates with nonstick cooking oil.
2.Toss the turkey with salt, black pepper, and olive oil. Divide the chicken pieces between both drawers.
3.Select zone 1 and pair it with "ROAST" at 180°C for 50 minutes. Select "MATCH" to duplicate settings across both zones. Press the "START/STOP" button.
4.At the halfway point, gently turn the turkey pieces over and reinsert the drawers to resume cooking.
5.Meanwhile, mix all the sauce Ingredients until well combined. Divide the turkey between tortillas; top with 50 grams of cheese and roll tightly to assemble your enchiladas.
6.Divide enchiladas between two lightly greased baking tins; spoon the sauce over them and sprinkle over the remaining 50 grams of cheese; add them to both drawers (without crisper plates).
7.Select zone 1 and pair it with "BAKE" at 190°C for 13 minutes, until golden brown on the top. Select "MATCH" to duplicate settings across both zones. Press the "START/STOP" button. Bon appétit!
Per Serving:
Calories: 665g / Fat: 42.1g / Carbs: 3.3g /
Fibre: 2.8g / Protein: 35.3g

Moroccan Turkey Salad

Prep time: 10 minutes / Cook time: 50 minutes / Serves 5

Ingredients

- 600g turkey breasts, skinless and boneless
- 1 medium aubergine, peeled and sliced
- 1 tsp cayenne pepper
- 1 tsp mustard powder
- Sea salt and ground black pepper, to taste
- 2 tbsp extra-virgin olive oil
- 2 spring onions, sliced
- 1 large tomato, diced
- 1 small cucumber, peeled and diced
- 1 small head of lettuce

Instructions

1. Toss the turkey breasts and aubergine with cooking oil and spices in a resealable bag; give them a good shake until everything is well covered.
2. Lower the turkey breasts into the zone 1 drawer and the aubergine into the zone 2 drawer,
3. Select zone 1 and pair it with "AIR FRY" at 180°C for 50 minutes. Select zone 2 and pair it with "ROAST" at 200°C for 8 minutes. Select "SYNC" followed by the "START/STOP" button.
4. At the half point, turn your Ingredients over to promote even cooking. Reinsert drawers to resume cooking.
5. Cut the turkey breasts into strips and add them to a salad bowl. Add the remaining ingredients, including the roasted aubergine, to the salad; gently stir to combine.
6. Bon appétit!

Per Serving:
Calories: 265g / Fat: 14.3g / Carbs: 4.4g / Fibre: 1.5g / Protein: 27.3g

Spicy Turkey Pasta Bake

Prep time: 5 minutes / Cook time: 40 minutes / Serves 6

Ingredients

- 400g pasta, dry
- 600g turkey mince
- 200g bacon lardons
- 1 tbsp olive oil
- 2 medium ripe tomatoes, chopped
- 200ml vegetable broth
- Sea salt and ground black pepper, to taste
- 1 tsp paprika
- 1 medium leek, chopped
- 1 medium celery, chopped
- 1 medium carrot, chopped
- 100g cheddar, grated

Instructions

1. Boil your pasta following pack Instructions; drain and reserve.
2. Add all the ingredients, except the cheese, to a large bowl and stir until everything is well combined.
3. Spoon the mixture into two lightly greased baking trays. Add the baking trays to the drawers (without crisper plates).
4. Select zone 1 and pair it with "BAKE" at 180°C for 40 minutes. Select "MATCH" followed by the "START/STOP" button.
5. At the halfway point, gently stir the Ingredients using a wooden spoon. Top with cheese and reinsert drawers to resume cooking.
6. Bon appétit!

Per Serving:
Calories: 635g / Fat: 30.3g / Carbs: 58.4g / Fibre: 8.5g / Protein: 34.3g

Classic Chicken Risotto

Prep time: 10 minutes / Cook time: 30 minutes / Serves 4

Ingredients

- 600g chicken, boneless and skinless, chopped
- 2 tbsp olive oil
- 1 tsp poultry spice mix
- 1 onion, chopped
- 2 garlic cloves, crushed or finely chopped
- 1 (400g) can tomatoes, chopped
- 600ml hot chicken stock

- 200g basmati rice

Instructions

1. Toss the chicken with olive oil and poultry spice mix. Add the other Ingredients and mix to combine well.
2. Divide the mixture between two baking trays. Add baking trays to the drawers and cover them with a double layer of foil.
3. Select zone 1 and pair it with "AIR FRY" at 190°C for 30 minutes. Select "MATCH" to duplicate settings across both zones. Press the "START/STOP" button.
4. At the halfway point, remove the foil and reinsert the drawers to resume cooking.
5. Serve warm and enjoy!

Per Serving:
Calories: 455g / Fat: 10.8g / Carbs: 45.8g / Fibre: 2.8g / Protein: 40.1g

Turkey Traybake

Prep time: 5 minutes / Cook time: 45 minutes / Serves 4

Ingredients

- 600g turkey breasts, boneless and cut into 4 pieces
- 2 celery sticks, trimmed and cut into 1.5cm pieces
- 2 medium carrots, trimmed and cut into 1.5cm pieces
- 2 medium leeks, quartered
- 1 tbsp olive oil
- 1/2 tsp hot paprika
- 1 tsp garlic granules
- Sea salt and ground black pepper, to taste

Instructions

1. Insert a crisper plate into the zone 1 drawer. Spray the crisper plate with nonstick cooking oil.
2. Toss the turkey and vegetables with spices and olive oil until they are well coated on all sides.
3. Place the turkey in the zone 1 drawer. Arrange the vegetable in a lightly greased roasting tin; add the roasting tin to the zone 2 drawer (with no crisper plate inserted).
4. Select zone 1 and pair it with "AIR FRY" at 180°C for 45 minutes. Select zone 2 and pair it with "ROAST" at 200°C for 12 minutes. Select "SYNC" followed by the "START/STOP" button.
5. When zone 1 time reaches 22 minutes, turn the turkey breasts over and spray them with nonstick cooking oil on the other side; reinsert the drawer to continue cooking
6. When zone 2 time reaches 6 minutes, stir the vegetables and reinsert the drawer to continue cooking.
7. Top the turkey breasts with vegetables and serve from the tray in the middle of the table.
8. Bon appétit!

Per Serving:
Calories: 320g / Fat: 14.2g / Carbs: 12.2g / Fibre: 2.8g / Protein: 34.4g

Easy Chicken Frittata

Prep time: 10 minutes / Cook time: 15 minutes / Serves 4

Ingredients

- 400g boneless chicken breasts, chopped
- 7 large eggs, beaten
- 1 medium onion, chopped
- 2 garlic cloves, minced
- 2 tbsp fresh cilantro, chopped
- 1 tsp hot paprika
- Sea salt and ground black pepper, to taste

Instructions

1. Grease two baking trays with cooking oil.
2. In a mixing bowl, thoroughly combine all the ingredients. Spoon the mixture into the baking trays.
3. Lower them into the drawers (without crisper plates).
4. Select zone 1 and pair it with "BAKE" at 180°C for 15 minutes. Select "MATCH" followed by the "START/STOP" button.
5. Cut each frittata into wedges and serve immediately. Bon appétit!

Per Serving:
Calories: 317g / Fat: 17.7g / Carbs: 5.1g /
Fibre: 0.9g / Protein: 32.5g

Chicken Nuggets

Prep time: 10 minutes + marinating time /
Cook time: 18 minutes / Serves 4

Ingredients
- 600g chicken breast, cut into bite-sized pieces
- 100ml natural yoghurt
- Sea salt and ground black pepper, to taste
- 1 tsp paprika
- 100g cornflakes, crushed
- 1 tbsp olive oil

Instructions
1. Mix the chicken pieces with yoghurt, salt, black pepper, and paprika in a ceramic bowl. Leave it to marinate in your fridge for about 3 hours.
2. Discard the marinade and press each piece of the marinated chicken onto the crushed cornflakes, pressing to adhere. Brush the chicken pieces with olive oil and arrange them in the cooking basket.
3. Select zone 1 and pair it with "AIR FRY" at 200°C for 18 minutes. Select "MATCH" to duplicate settings across both zones. Press the "START/STOP" button.
4. When zone 1 time reaches 9 minutes, shake the basket to ensure even cooking. Reinsert the drawers to continue cooking.
5. Enjoy!
Per Serving:
Calories: 401g / Fat: 19.4g / Carbs: 21.1g /
Fibre: 2.2g / Protein: 34.8g

Asian-Style Duck Salad

Prep time: 5 minutes / Cook time: 20 minutes /
Serves 4

Ingredients
- 600 duck breasts, boneless and cut into 2 pieces
- 1 tbsp butter, room temperature
- 2 tbsp soy sauce
- 2 tbsp rice vinegar
- 1 tsp Five-spice powder
- 400g punnet cherry tomatoes
- 2 tbsp extra-virgin olive oil
- 1 small cucumber, sliced
- 1 medium bell pepper, sliced

Instructions
1. Pat the duck breasts dry with kitchen paper.
2. In a mixing bowl, toss the duck breasts with the butter, soy sauce, rice vinegar, and Five-spice powder.
3. Add the duck to the zone 1 drawer and punnet cherry tomatoes to the zone 2 drawer. Brush tomatoes with cooking oil.
4. Select zone 1 and pair it with "ROAST" at 195°C for 20 minutes. Select zone 2 and pair it with "ROAST" at 200°C for 8 minutes. Select "SYNC" followed by the "START/STOP" button.
5. At the half point, turn your Ingredients over to promote even cooking. Reinsert drawers to resume cooking.
6. Cut duck breasts into strips and add them to a salad bowl; add the other Ingredients and toss to combine.
7. Bon appétit!
Per Serving:
Calories: 333g / Fat: 17.9g / Carbs: 7.8g /
Fibre: 2g / Protein: 31.8g

Cheesy Spicy Chicken Fillets

Prep time: 10 minutes / Cook time: 19 minutes
/ Serves 5

Ingredients
- 1kg chicken fillets
- 1 tsp olive oil
- 1 tsp hot paprika
- Sea salt and ground black pepper, to taste
- 50g cream cheese
- 50g cheddar cheese, grated
- 50ml chicken stock

Instructions
1. Toss chicken breast fillets with olive oil,

paprika, salt, and black pepper. Add the chicken fillets to baking tins and add them to both drawers.

2. Then, mix the remaining Ingredients until everything is well incorporated.

3. Select zone 1 and pair it with "BAKE" at 190°C for 19 minutes. Select "MATCH" followed by the "START/STOP" button.

4. When zone 1 time reaches 10 minutes, turn the chicken fillets over and top them with the cheese mixture; reinsert the drawers to continue cooking.

5. Serve warm and enjoy!

Per Serving:

Calories: 407g / Fat: 23.8g / Carbs: 1.7g / Fibre: 0.2g / Protein: 43.9g

Glazed Mini Meatloaves

Prep time: 10 minutes / Cook time: 20 minutes / Serves 4

Ingredients
* Meatloaves:
* 600g turkey breasts, chopped
* 100g bacon lardons
* 1 garlic clove, minced
* 1 medium onion, chopped
* Sea salt and ground black pepper, to taste
* 2 medium eggs, beaten
* 100g sharp cheese, grated
* Glaze:
* 200ml tomato paste
* 1 tbsp clear honey
* 1 tbsp English mustard

Instructions
1. Brush four ramekins with nonstick cooking oil.
2. In a mixing bowl, thoroughly combine all the Ingredients for mini meatloaves. Scrape the mixture into the prepared ramekins.
3. Select zone 1 and pair it with "AIR FRY" at 180°C for 20 minutes. Select "MATCH" to duplicate settings across both zones. Press the "START/STOP" button.
4. When zone 1 time reaches 10 minutes, top

them with the glaze mixture; reinsert the drawers to continue cooking.

5. Devour!

Per Serving:

Calories: 517g / Fat: 28.2g / Carbs: 20.4g / Fibre: 2.9g / Protein: 45.7g

Chicken Quinoa Pilaf

Prep time: 10 minutes / Cook time: 35 minutes / Serves 4

Ingredients
* 600g turkey, boneless and skinless, chopped
* 2 tbsp olive oil
* 1 tsp poultry spice mix
* 1 onion, chopped
* 2 garlic cloves, crushed or finely chopped
* 1 (400g) can tomatoes, chopped
* 600ml hot chicken stock
* 200g quinoa, drained and rinsed

Instructions
1. Toss the turkey with olive oil and poultry spice mix. Add the other Ingredients and mix to combine well.
2. Divide the mixture between two baking trays. Add baking trays to the drawers and cover them with a double layer of foil.
3. Select zone 1 and pair it with "AIR FRY" at 190°C for 35 minutes. Select "MATCH" to duplicate settings across both zones. Press the "START/STOP" button.
4. At the halfway point, remove the foil and reinsert the drawers to resume cooking.
5. Serve warm and enjoy!

Per Serving:

Calories: 457g / Fat: 14.1g / Carbs: 37.3g / Fibre: 4.9g / Protein: 45.7g

Poultry Keto Pie

Prep time: 10 minutes / Cook time: 23 minutes / Serves 4

Ingredients
* 400g cauliflower florets
* 400g ground chicken

- 100g bacon lardons
- 4 large eggs, beaten
- 1 medium onion, chopped
- 2 garlic cloves, minced
- 2 tbsp fresh cilantro, chopped
- 1 tsp hot paprika
- Sea salt and ground black pepper, to taste

Instructions

1. Cook cauliflower florets at 200°C for 8 minutes. Now, mash your cauliflower with a potato masher or food processor.
2. Grease two baking trays with cooking oil.
3. In a mixing bowl, thoroughly combine all the ingredients, including the cauliflower mash. Spoon the mixture into the baking trays.
4. Lower them into the drawers (without crisper plates).
5. Select zone 1 and pair it with "BAKE" at 190°C for 15 minutes. Select "MATCH" followed by the "START/STOP" button.
6. Cut your pies into wedges and serve immediately. Bon appétit!

Per Serving:

Calories: 357g / Fat: 23.1g / Carbs: 8.9g / Fibre: 2.7g / Protein: 29.2g

Turkey Burgers

Prep time: 10 minutes / Cook time: 25 minutes / Serves 5

Ingredients

- 600g turkey mince
- 200g pork mince
- 1 medium onion, chopped
- 2 garlic cloves, minced
- 60g fresh breadcrumbs
- Sea salt and ground black pepper, to taste
- 1 tsp cayenne pepper
- 1 tsp mustard powder
- 5 burger buns
- 1 small head of lettuce leaves
- 1 tbsp mustard
- 1 medium tomato, diced
- 2 spring onions, sliced

- 50ml mayonnaise

Instructions

1. Insert a crisper plate in each drawer. Spray the crisper plates with nonstick cooking oil.
2. Thoroughly combine the meat, onion, garlic, breadcrumbs, and spices. Shape the mixture into five patties.
3. Add burgers to each drawer and spray them with cooking oil.
4. Select zone 1 and pair it with "AIR FRY" at 190°C for 25 minutes. Select "MATCH" to duplicate settings across both zones. Press the "START/STOP" button.
5. When zone 1 time reaches 10 minutes, turn the burgers over and spray them with cooking oil on the other side. Reinsert the drawers to continue cooking.
6. Serve your burgers in the buns topped with tomatoes, spring onions, and mayonnaise.
7. Bon appétit!

Per Serving:

Calories: 552g / Fat: 24g / Carbs: 45.4g / Fibre: 4.9g / Protein: 38.9g

Asian-Style Maple Duck

Prep time: 5 minutes / Cook time: 25 minutes / Serves 5

Ingredients

- 1kg duck breasts, boneless and cut into 2 pieces
- 2 tbsp rice vinegar
- 1 tbsp maple syrup
- 2 tbsp tamari sauce
- 1 tbsp sesame oil, lightly toasted
- 1 tsp red pepper flakes
- Sea salt and ground black pepper, to taste

Instructions

1. Pat the duck breasts dry with kitchen paper.
2. Add the duck breasts and the other Ingredients to a bag. Give it a good shake and add the duck breasts to the cooking basket.
3. Select zone 1 and pair it with "ROAST" at 195°C for 10 minutes. Select "MATCH" to

duplicate settings across both zones. Press the "START/STOP" button.

4. When the time is up, turn the temperature down to 160°C, and continue to cook the duck for a further 15 minutes.

5. Bon appétit!

Per Serving:

Calories: 288g / Fat: 11.2g / Carbs: 4.4g / Fibre: 0.4g / Protein: 40g

Thanksgiving Roast Turkey

Prep time: 5 minutes / Cook time: 1 hour / Serves 4

Ingredients

- 1kg turkey breasts, skin-on, boneless, cut into two pieces
- 30g butter, at room temperature
- 1 bay leaf
- 1 rosemary sprig, leaves finely chopped
- 2 garlic cloves, crushed
- 1 tbsp English mustard
- Sea salt and ground black pepper, to taste

Instructions

1. Insert crisper plates in both drawers. Spray the crisper plates with nonstick cooking oil.
2. Pat turkey breasts dry with tea towels. Crush the spices and garlic using a pestle and mortar.
3. Rub turkey all over with the butter and spice mix. Lower turkey breasts onto the prepared crisper plates.
4. Select zone 1 and pair it with "ROAST" at 200°C for 1 hour. Select "MATCH" to duplicate settings across both zones. Press the "START/STOP" button.
5. At the halfway point, turn the turkey breasts over to promote even cooking; reinsert the drawers to resume cooking.
6. Bon appétit!

Per Serving:

Calories: 455g / Fat: 23.7g / Carbs: 1.8g / Fibre: 0.4g / Protein: 55.2g

Cheese Duck Patties

Prep time: 10 minutes / Cook time: 25 minutes / Serves 6

Ingredients

- 600g duck breasts, skinless, boneless and chopped
- 200g cheddar cheese, grated
- 1 medium onion, chopped
- 2 garlic cloves, minced
- 100g breadcrumbs
- Sea salt and ground black pepper, to taste
- 1 tsp mustard powder
- 1 tsp smoked paprika

Instructions

1. Insert a crisper plate in each drawer. Spray the crisper plates with nonstick cooking oil.
2. Thoroughly combine the Ingredients and shape the mixture into six patties.
3. Add the patties to each drawer and spray them with cooking oil.
4. Select zone 1 and pair it with "AIR FRY" at 190°C for 25 minutes. Select "MATCH" to duplicate settings across both zones. Press the "START/STOP" button.
5. When zone 1 time reaches 10 minutes, turn the patties over and spray them with cooking oil on the other side. Reinsert the drawers to continue cooking.
6. Bon appétit!

Per Serving:

Calories: 316g / Fat: 16.2g / Carbs: 11.6g / Fibre: 1.1g / Protein: 29.8g

Roast Turkey Leg with New Potatoes

Prep time: 10 minutes / Cook time: 55 minutes / Serves 4

Ingredients

- 600g turkey leg, boneless
- 600g new potatoes, chopped
- 2 garlic cloves, crushed or finely chopped
- 1 thyme sprig, chopped

- 1 rosemary sprig
- 2 tsp olive oil

Instructions

1. Pat the turkey leg dry with tea towels. Crush the spices and garlic using a pestle and mortar.
2. Rub turkey and potatoes with olive oil and spice mix. Lower turkey leg into the zone drawer and potatoes into the zone 2 drawer.
3. Select zone 1 and pair it with "ROAST" at 185°C for 55 minutes. Select zone 2 and pair it with "ROAST" at 190°C for 20 minutes. Select "SYNC" followed by the "START/STOP" button.
4. At the half point, turn your Ingredients over to promote even cooking. Reinsert drawers to resume cooking.
5. Bon appétit!

Per Serving:
Calories: 356g / Fat: 12.4g / Carbs: 26g / Fibre: 3.3g / Protein: 32.4g

Old-Fashioned Turkey Casserole

Prep time: 10 minutes / Cook time: 55 minutes / Serves 4

Ingredients

- 500g turkey breast, boneless and skinless, chopped
- 500g potatoes, chopped
- 2 small leeks, quartered
- 2 carrots, sliced
- 2 celery stalks, sliced
- 2 garlic cloves, crushed or finely chopped
- 1 thyme sprig, chopped
- 200ml hot vegetable stock
- 2 tbsp olive oil

Instructions

1. Add all the other Ingredients to a mixing bowl and mix to combine well.
2. Divide the mixture between two baking tins. Add baking tins to the drawers and cover them with a double layer of foil.
3. Select zone 1 and pair it with "AIR FRY" at 180°C for 55 minutes. Select "MATCH" to duplicate settings across both zones. Press the "START/STOP" button.
4. At the halfway point, remove the foil and reinsert the drawers to resume cooking. Bon appétit!

Per Serving:
Calories: 396g / Fat: 16.2g / Carbs: 29g / Fibre: 3.8g / Protein: 31.9g

Turkey Patties

Prep time: 10 minutes / Cook time: 25 minutes / Serves 5

Ingredients

- 600g turkey mince
- 100g bacon lardons
- 1 medium onion, chopped
- 2 garlic cloves, minced
- 100g tortilla chips, crushed
- 1 tsp cayenne pepper
- 1 tsp mustard powder
- Sea salt and ground black pepper, to taste
- 5 burger buns
- 1 small head of lettuce leaves
- 1 tbsp mustard
- 1 medium tomato, diced
- 2 spring onions, sliced
- 50ml mayonnaise

Instructions

1. Insert a crisper plate in each drawer. Spray the crisper plates with nonstick cooking oil.
2. In a mixing bowl, combine turkey mince, bacon, onion, garlic, tortilla chips, and spices. Shape the mixture into four patties.
3. Add burgers to each drawer and spray them with cooking oil.
4. Select zone 1 and pair it with "AIR FRY" at 190°C for 25 minutes. Select "MATCH" to duplicate settings across both zones. Press the "START/STOP" button.
5. When zone 1 time reaches 10 minutes, turn the burgers over and spray them with cooking

oil on the other side. Reinsert the drawers to continue cooking.

6. Serve your burgers in the buns topped with lettuce, mustard, tomatoes, spring onions, and mayonnaise.

7. Bon appétit!

Per Serving:
Calories: 546g / Fat: 21g / Carbs: 51.1g / Fibre: 5.5g / Protein: 38.3g

Turkey Millet Bake

Prep time: 10 minutes / Cook time: 35 minutes / Serves 6

Ingredients

- 500g turkey mince
- 1 tsp poultry spice mix
- 100g pancetta, cut into bite-sized pieces
- 1 tbsp olive oil
- 1 onion, chopped
- 2 garlic cloves, crushed or finely chopped
- 1 medium bell pepper, deseeded and sliced
- 1 (400g) can tomatoes, chopped
- 600ml hot chicken stock
- 200g quinoa, drained and rinsed

Instructions

1. Toss the turkey mince with the poultry spice mix. Add the other Ingredients and stir to combine well.

2. Divide the mixture between two baking trays. Add baking trays to the drawers and cover them with a double layer of foil.

3. Select zone 1 and pair it with "AIR FRY" at 190°C for 35 minutes. Select "MATCH" to duplicate settings across both zones. Press the "START/STOP" button.

4. At the halfway point, remove the foil and reinsert the drawers to resume cooking.

5. Bon appétit!

Per Serving:
Calories: 376g / Fat: 18.2g / Carbs: 26.7g / Fibre: 4.4g / Protein: 26.3g

Turkey & Pepper Quiche

Prep time: 10 minutes / Cook time: 25 minutes / Serves 5

Ingredients

- 400g ground turkey
- 100g bacon lardons
- 200g cheddar cheese, grated
- 4 large eggs, beaten
- 1 medium bell pepper, deseeded and chopped
- 1 chilli pepper, deseeded and chopped
- 2 garlic cloves, minced
- 2 tbsp fresh chives, chopped
- 2 tbsp fresh parsley, chopped
- 1 tsp Italian spice mix
- Sea salt and ground black pepper, to taste

Instructions

1. Grease two baking trays with cooking oil.

2. In a mixing bowl, thoroughly combine all the ingredients. Divide the mixture between the prepared baking trays.

3. Lower them into the drawers (without crisper plates).

4. Select zone 1 and pair it with "BAKE" at 180°C for 25 minutes. Select "MATCH" followed by the "START/STOP" button.

5. Cut your quiche into wedges and serve immediately.

6. Bon appétit!

Per Serving:
Calories: 433g / Fat: 31.3g / Carbs: 1.1g / Fibre: 0.5g / Protein: 33.5g

CHAPTER 4 : MEAT

Roast Pork with Crackling

Prep time: 30 minutes + marinating time /
Cook time: 55 minutes / Serves 5

Ingredients
- 2 pieces of rolled and tied pork loin (1kg), skin scored
- 5 garlic cloves, peeled and cut into thin slivers
- 1 lemon, freshly squeezed
- 2 tbsp red wine
- 1 tbsp olive oil
- 1 tsp dried onion flakes
- 1 tsp dried rosemary
- 1 tsp dried parsley flakes
- 1 tsp cayenne pepper
- Sea salt and ground black pepper, to taste

Instructions
1. Using a small knife, stab through the fatty side of the pork loin to make 15-16 incisions. Now, insert a sliver of garlic into each stab mark.
2. Toss pork loin with the remaining ingredients. Leave the pork to marinate overnight in your fridge.
3. Remove the pork from the marinade and season it with salt and pepper to taste.
4. Select zone 1 and pair it with "AIR FRY" at 195°C for 55 minutes. Select "MATCH" to duplicate settings across both zones. Press the "START/STOP" button.
5. At the halfway point, shake the basket, baste the pork with the reserved marinade, and reinsert the drawers to resume cooking.
6. Leave the pork to rest for about 30 minutes before carving. Bon appétit!

Per Serving:
Calories: 377g / Fat: 20.9g / Carbs: 3.1g /
Fibre: 0.4g / Protein: 41.9g

Beef Curry

Prep time: 10 minutes / Cook time: 26 minutes
/ Serves 4

Ingredients
- 2 tsp olive oil
- 1 large onion, chopped
- 400g beef mince
- 1 tsp ginger-garlic paste
- 1 tsp turmeric powder
- 1 tsp garam masala
- 1 (400g) can tomatoes, chopped
- 100ml coconut milk
- 2 tbsp fresh cilantro, chopped

Instructions
1. Heat 1 teaspoon of olive oil in a frying pan over medium-high heat. Sauté the onion for about 3 minutes, until just tender.
2. Add beef mince and continue to cook for 3 minutes, until no longer pink.
3. Then, sauté the ginger-garlic paste for about 30 seconds, until fragrant.
4. Brush the inside of two oven-safe baking tins with the remaining 1 teaspoon of olive oil. Add the sauteed mixture along with the spices and tomatoes to the baking tins; gently stir to combine and lower them into the drawers.
5. Select zone 1 and pair it with "AIR FRY" at 180°C for 20 minutes. Select "MATCH" to duplicate settings across both zones. Press the "START/STOP" button.
6. When zone 1 time reaches 10 minutes, gently stir your curry and add the coconut milk; reinsert the drawers to continue cooking.
7. Garnish your curry with fresh cilantro. Devour!

Per Serving:
Calories: 317g / Fat: 20g / Carbs: 7.1g / Fibre:
2.3g / Protein: 28g

Easy Pork Burritos

Prep time: 10 minutes / Cook time: 55 minutes
/ Serves 5

Ingredients
- 1kg pork shoulder, cut into 4 pieces
- 1 tbsp olive oil

- 1 tsp mustard powder
- 1 tsp garlic granules
- 1 tsp onion powder
- Sea salt and ground black pepper, to taste
- 3 tbsp tomato paste
- 100ml chicken broth
- 1 jalapeño pepper, deveined
- 5 medium tortillas
- 500g cooked rice
- 200g can black beans, drained and rinsed

Instructions

1. Insert crisper plates in zone 1 and 2 drawers. Spray the crisper plates with nonstick cooking oil.
2. Toss pork shoulder with olive oil and spices. Divide the pork shoulder between both drawers.
3. Select zone 1 and pair it with "ROAST" at 175°C for 55 minutes. Select "MATCH" to duplicate settings across both zones. Press the "START/STOP" button.
4. At the halfway point, turn the pork pieces over and reinsert the drawers to resume cooking.
5. Shred the pork with two forks and divide it between tortillas; add the other Ingredients and roll them up.
6. Add burritos to the drawers. Select zone 1 and pair it with "REHEAT" at 160°C for 5 minutes. Enjoy!

Per Serving:
Calories: 587g / Fat: 17.5g / Carbs: 59.1g / Fibre: 3.2g / Protein: 45.4g

Hearty Cheeseburger Casserole

Prep time: 5 minutes / Cook time: 40 minutes / Serves 5

Ingredients

- 1 tbsp olive oil
- 800g beef mince
- 100ml tomato puree
- 100ml chicken broth
- 1 tbsp beef bouillon granules
- Sea salt and ground black pepper, to taste
- 1 tsp paprika
- 1 small leek, peeled and chopped

- 1 celery stalk, chopped
- 1 medium carrot, chopped
- 150g gruyere cheese, crumbled

Instructions

1. Add all the ingredients, except the cheese, to a large bowl and stir until everything is well combined.
2. Spoon the mixture into two lightly greased baking tins. Add the baking tins to the drawers (without crisper plates).
3. Select zone 1 and pair it with "ROAST" at 180°C for 40 minutes. Select "MATCH" followed by the "START/STOP" button.
4. At the halfway point, gently stir the Ingredients using a wooden spoon. Top your casserole with cheese and reinsert drawers to resume cooking.
5. Bon appétit!

Per Serving:
Calories: 527g / Fat: 30.7g / Carbs: 7.8g / Fibre: 1.4g / Protein: 53.1g

Hungarian Beef Goulash

Prep time: 10 minutes / Cook time: 28 minutes / Serves 4

Ingredients

- 2 tsp olive oil
- 1 large onion, chopped
- 600g stewing steak, cut into chunks
- 2 garlic cloves, crushed
- 1 tsp turmeric powder
- 1 tbsp paprika
- 2 tbsp tomato purée
- 2 large tomatoes, diced
- 300ml beef broth

Instructions

1. Heat 1 teaspoon of olive oil in a frying pan over medium-high heat. Sauté the onion for about 3 minutes, until just tender.
2. Add the steak and continue to cook for 3 minutes, until no longer pink.
3. Then, sauté the garlic for about 30 seconds, until fragrant.
4. Brush the inside of two oven-safe baking tins with the remaining 1 teaspoon of olive oil. Add

the sauteed mixture along with the remaining Ingredients to the baking tins; gently stir to combine and lower them into the drawers.

5. Select zone 1 and pair it with "AIR FRY" at 180°C for 22 minutes. Select "MATCH" to duplicate settings across both zones. Press the "START/STOP" button.

6. When zone 1 time reaches 11 minutes, gently stir your goulash and reinsert the drawers to continue cooking.

7. Serve warm and enjoy!

Per Serving:
Calories: 287g / Fat: 12.5g / Carbs: 10.2g / Fibre: 2.7g / Protein: 34.4g

Pork Hot Pot

Prep time: 10 minutes + marinating time / Cook time: 25 minutes / Serves 5

Ingredients
* 800g pork tenderloin, cut into bite-sized pieces
* 1 tbsp olive oil
* 1 tsp garlic, crushed
* 1 chilli pepper, minced
* 100ml red wine
* 100ml chicken stock
* 2 tbsp plain flour
* 1 medium onion, peeled and sliced
* 1 large carrot, trimmed and sliced
* 2 bell peppers, seeded and sliced
* 2 garlic cloves, finely sliced

Instructions
1. Place the pork tenderloin, olive oil, garlic, chilli pepper, and wine in a ceramic or glass dish; cover the dish and allow the pork to marinate for approximately 2 hours in your fridge. Discard the marinade.

2. Toss the pork pieces with plain flour and add them to the lightly greased baking tin.

3. Add the other Ingredients to the baking tin. Gently stir to combine and cover the baking trays with foil (with the shiny side down). Place the baking trays in both drawers.

4. Select zone 1 and pair it with "AIR FRY" at 185°C for 25 minutes. Select "MATCH" to duplicate settings across both zones. Press the "START/STOP" button.

5. Enjoy!

Per Serving:
Calories: 297g / Fat: 8.7g / Carbs: 8.7g / Fibre: 1.2g / Protein: 43.4g

Pork Carnitas

Prep time: 10 minutes / Cook time: 55 minutes / Serves 4

Ingredients
* 1kg pork shoulder, cut into 4 pieces
* 1 tbsp olive oil
* 1 tsp onion powder
* 1 tsp mustard powder
* 1 tsp garlic granules
* 1 tsp Mexican oregano
* Sea salt and ground black pepper, to taste
* 2 tbsp lemon juice
* 100ml chicken broth
* 3 tbsp tomato puree
* 1 jalapeño pepper, deveined

Instructions
1. Insert crisper plates in zone 1 and 2 drawers. Spray the crisper plates with nonstick cooking oil.

2. Toss pork shoulder with olive oil and spices. Divide the pork pieces between both drawers.

3. Meanwhile, mix the remaining Ingredients to make the sauce for your carnitas.

4. Select zone 1 and pair it with "ROAST" at 175°C for 55 minutes. Select "MATCH" to duplicate settings across both zones. Press the "START/STOP" button.

5. At the halfway point, turn the pork pieces over and baste them with the prepared sauce; reinsert the drawers to resume cooking.

6. Shred the pork with two forks and serve the shredded pork in corn tortillas.

7. Bon appétit!

Per Serving:
Calories: 379g / Fat: 17.8g / Carbs: 4.7g /

Fibre: 0.8g / Protein: 47.6g

Steak & Aubergine Salad

Prep time: 10 minutes / Cook time: 20 minutes / Serves 4

Ingredients

- 500g skirt steak, sliced
- 500g aubergine, sliced
- 2 tbsp extra-virgin olive oil
- 2 garlic cloves, crushed
- Sea salt and ground black pepper, to taste
- 1 large tomato, diced
- 1 small cucumber, sliced
- 1 medium onion, sliced
- 2 tbsp fresh lemon juice

Instructions

1. Toss the steak and aubergine with 1 tablespoon of olive oil, garlic, salt, and black pepper.
2. Place the steak in the zone 1 drawer. Place aubergine slices in the zone 2 drawer.
3. Select zone 1 and pair it with "AIR FRY" at 195°C for 20 minutes. Select zone 2 and pair it with "ROAST" at 200°C for 8 minutes. Select "SYNC" followed by the "START/STOP" button.
4. At the half point, turn your Ingredients over to promote even cooking. Reinsert drawers to resume cooking.
5. Cut the steak into bite-sized strips and add them to a salad bowl; add the other Ingredients and toss to combine.
6. Bon appétit!

Per Serving:
Calories: 288g / Fat: 14.5g / Carbs: 12.5g / Fibre: 4.8g / Protein: 27.4g

Pork Chop Melts

Prep time: 5 minutes / Cook time: 16 minutes / Serves 4

Ingredients

- 1 kg good quality pork chops
- 1 tbsp butter, melted
- 1 tsp cayenne pepper
- Sea salt and ground black pepper, to taste
- 2 tbsp applesauce, unsweetened
- 120g stilton cheese, crumbled

Instructions

1. Insert crisper plates in both drawers. Spray the crisper plates with nonstick cooking oil.
2. Toss pork chops with butter and spices; now, lower them into the cooking basket.
3. Select zone 1 and pair it with "AIR FRY" at 200°C for 16 minutes. Select "MATCH" to duplicate settings across both zones. Press the "START/STOP" button.
4. At the halfway point, turn the pork chops over and top them with applesauce and then cheese; reinsert the drawers to resume cooking.
5. Bon appétit!

Per Serving:
Calories: 438g / Fat: 18.6g / Carbs: 4.8g / Fibre: 0.4g / Protein: 60.2g

Easy Sticky Ribs

Prep time: 5 minutes + marinating time / Cook time: 40 minutes / Serves 4

Ingredients

- 1kg spare ribs, cut between the bones
- 2 tbsp soy sauce
- 2 tbsp honey
- 100ml rice wine
- 100ml tomato sauce
- 1 tsp red pepper flakes
- Sea salt and ground black pepper, to taste

Instructions

1. Add the ribs and the other Ingredients to a glass bowl; cover the bowl and allow the ribs to marinate for approximately 2 hours in your fridge. Reserve the marinade.
2. Arrange the ribs in two roasting trays and lower them into both drawers.
3. Select zone 1 and pair it with "AIR FRY" at 180°C for 40 minutes. Select "MATCH" to duplicate settings across both zones. Press the "START/STOP" button.
4. At the halfway point, turn the ribs over and baste them with the reserved marinade; reinsert

the drawers to resume cooking.

5. Bon appétit!

Per Serving:
Calories: 550g / Fat: 28.1g / Carbs: 16.8g / Fibre: 1.8g / Protein: 52.2g

Pulled Pork Tacos

Prep time: 10 minutes / Cook time: 55 minutes / Serves 4

Ingredients
- 1kg pork shoulder, cut into 2 pieces
- 100ml tomato sauce
- 1 tbsp olive oil
- 1 tsp taco spice mix
- Sea salt and ground black pepper, to taste
- 1 small onion, sliced
- 4 bell peppers, deseeded and halved
- 4 medium tortillas

Instructions
1. Toss pork shoulder with tomato sauce, olive oil and spices. Add the pork shoulder to the zone 1 drawer and bell peppers to the zone 2 drawer.
2. Select zone 1 and pair it with "ROAST" at 175°C for 55 minutes. Select zone 2 and pair it with "ROAST" at 180°C for 15 minutes. Select "SYNC" followed by the "START/STOP" button.
3. At the halfway point, turn the pork pieces over and baste them with the remaining sauce; reinsert the drawers to resume cooking.
4. Turn the peppers 2 to 3 times during the cooking process. Once cooking is complete, cut the peppers into strips.
5. Shred the pork with two forks. Pile into tortillas along with roasted peppers and onions. Enjoy!

Per Serving:
Calories: 561g / Fat: 20.7g / Carbs: 37.4g / Fibre: 3.8g / Protein: 52.2g

Beef Brisket Pot Roast

Prep time: 10 minutes + marinating time / Cook time: 45 minutes / Serves 4

Ingredients
- 600g rolled beef brisket

- 1 tbsp soy sauce
- 100ml red wine
- 1 tbsp English mustard
- 2 bay leaves
- 1 sprig of rosemary, chopped
- Sea salt and ground black pepper, to taste
- 2 tbsp corn flour
- 2 tsp vegetable oil
- 2 large carrots, trimmed and cut into bite-sized pieces
- 2 bell peppers, deseeded and halved

Instructions
1. Place the beef, soy sauce, wine, mustard, bay leaves, and rosemary in a ceramic bowl; cover the bowl and allow the beef brisket to marinate for approximately 2 hours in your fridge. Reserve the marinade.
2. Toss the beef pieces with corn flour, 1 teaspoon of vegetable oil, salt, and pepper; add them to a lightly greased baking tray.
3. Toss the vegetables with the remaining 1 teaspoon of vegetable oil, salt, and black pepper. Add the vegetables to another baking tray and cover it with foil (with the shiny side down). Place the baking trays in both drawers.
4. Select zone 1 and pair it with "AIR FRY" at 180°C for 45 minutes. Select zone 2 and pair it with "ROAST" at 190°C for 12 minutes. Select "SYNC" followed by the "START/STOP" button.
5. When zone 1 time reaches 20 minutes, turn the beef over and reinsert the drawer to resume cooking
6. When zone 2 time reaches 6 minutes, turn your vegetables over to ensure even cooking and reinsert the drawer to resume cooking.
7. Meanwhile, make the sauce: gently simmer the marinade Ingredients over medium-high heat for about 10 minutes, until the sauce has thickened.
8. Arrange beef brisket with vegetables on a serving platter; spoon the sauce over them, and enjoy!

Per Serving:
Calories: 321g / Fat: 14.5g / Carbs: 12.4g / Fibre: 2.8g / Protein: 33.1g

Spicy Peppery Meatloaves

Prep time: 10 minutes / Cook time: 25 minutes / Serves 6

Ingredients

- 300g pork mince
- 300g beef mince
- 100g bacon lardons
- 50g fresh white breadcrumbs
- 50g parmesan, grated
- 1 bell pepper, deseeded and chopped
- 1 onion, chopped
- 2 garlic cloves, minced
- Sea salt and ground black pepper, to taste

Instructions

1. Brush two loaf tins with nonstick cooking oil. In a small bowl, mix 25 grams of the breadcrumbs and 25 grams of parmesan; set aside.
2. Then, thoroughly combine the remaining Ingredients for your meatloaves.
3. Scrape the mixture into the prepared loaf tins. Sprinkle with the reserved crumb/parmesan mixture.
4. Spray the top of your meatloaves with cooking oil. Add a loaf tin to each drawer.
5. Select zone 1 and pair it with "AIR FRY" at 180°C for 25 minutes. Select "MATCH" to duplicate settings across both zones. Press the "START/STOP" button.
6. Let your meatloaves sit for approximately 10 minutes before slicing and serving.
7. Bon appétit!

Per Serving:
Calories: 371g / Fat: 22.9g / Carbs: 7.2g / Fibre: 0.6g / Protein: 32.1g

Sunday Roast

Prep time: 10 minutes / Cook time: 55 minutes / Serves 4

Ingredients

- 600g beef rump roast, cut into 2 pieces
- 600g potatoes, peeled and cut into wedges
- 1 tbsp olive oil
- 2 garlic cloves, crushed
- 1 tsp dried rosemary
- 1 tsp cayenne pepper
- Sea salt and ground black pepper, to taste
- 4 Yorkshire pudding (optional)

Instructions

1. Toss the beef and potatoes with olive oil, garlic, and spices. Place the beef in the zone 1 drawer and the potatoes in the zone 2 drawer.
2. Select zone 1 and pair it with "ROAST" at 195°C for 55 minutes. Select zone 2 and pair it with "ROAST" at 190°C for 20 minutes. Select "SYNC" followed by the "START/STOP" button.
3. At the half point, turn your Ingredients over to promote even cooking. Reinsert drawers to resume cooking.
4. Bon appétit!

Per Serving:
Calories: 338g / Fat: 9.7g / Carbs: 28.1g / Fibre: 3.6g / Protein: 35.8g

Pork Fajitas

Prep time: 10 minutes / Cook time: 30 minutes / Serves 4

Ingredients

- 500g pork tenderloin, skinless, boneless, cut into strips
- 2 large bell pepper, deseeded and halved
- 1 medium onion, peeled and quartered
- 2 tbsp olive oil
- 1 tsp dried Mexican oregano
- Sea salt and freshly ground black pepper, to taste
- 1 chilli pepper, minced
- 4 medium corn tortillas

Instructions

1. Insert crisper plates in both drawers. Spray the crisper plates with nonstick cooking oil.
2. Toss pork tenderloin, peppers, and onion with olive oil and spices.
3. Place the pork tenderloin in the zone 1 drawer; place the peppers and onions in the zone 2 drawer.
4. Select zone 1 and pair it with "AIR FRY" at 195°C for 25 minutes. Select zone 2 and pair it with "ROAST" at 190°C for 15 minutes.

Select "SYNC" followed by the "START/STOP" button.

5. Shake the basket once or twice to promote even cooking. Reinsert the drawers to resume cooking.
6. Add tortillas to both drawers. Select "REHEAT" at 170°C for 5 minutes.
7. Add the pork to the warmed tortillas; top them with onions and peppers. Enjoy!

Per Serving:
Calories: 395g / Fat: 14.4g / Carbs: 33.8g / Fibre: 3.7g / Protein: 31.1g

Sticky Gammon Steaks

Prep time: 10 minutes / Cook time: 20 minutes / Serves 5

Ingredients
- 1kg gammon steaks
- 1 tsp dried parsley flakes
- 1 tsp dried onion flakes
- 1 tsp garlic granules
- 1 tsp cayenne pepper
- Sea salt and ground black pepper, to taste
- 1 tbsp olive oil
- 2 tbsp maple syrup

Instructions
1. Insert a crisper plate into the zone 1 and zone 2 drawers. Spray the crisper plates with nonstick cooking oil.
2. Toss gammon steaks with the other Ingredients and then, arrange them in zone 1 and zone 2 drawers.
3. Select zone 1 and pair it with "AIR FRY" at 180°C for 20 minutes. Select "MATCH" to duplicate settings across both zones. Press the "START/STOP" button.
4. At the halfway point, turn the gammon steaks over and reinsert the drawers to resume cooking.
5. Bon appétit!

Per Serving:
Calories: 423g / Fat: 27.5g / Carbs: 6.8g / Fibre: 0.3g / Protein: 35.1g

Sauerkraut with Pork Sausage

Prep time: 10 minutes / Cook time: 22 minutes / Serves 5

Ingredients
- 1 tbsp lard
- 2 onions, finely chopped
- 4 garlic cloves, crushed
- 1 bay leaf
- 800g pork sausages, casing removed
- 1 tbsp sweet paprika
- 100ml beef bone broth
- 400g white sauerkraut, squeezed and chopped (keep the pickling juice)

Instructions
1. Brush the inside of two baking trays with the melted lard.
2. Thoroughly combine all the Ingredients and divide them between two baking tins; gently stir to combine and lower them into the drawers.
3. Select zone 1 and pair it with "AIR FRY" at 190°C for 22 minutes. Select "MATCH" to duplicate settings across both zones. Press the "START/STOP" button.
4. When zone 1 time reaches 11 minutes, gently stir the Ingredients and reinsert the drawers to continue cooking.
5. Serve warm and enjoy!

Per Serving:
Calories: 467g / Fat: 31g / Carbs: 17.5g / Fibre: 4g / Protein: 27.1g

Pork Sausage and Vegetable Traybake

Prep time: 10 minutes / Cook time: 15 minutes / Serves 4

Ingredients
- 600g pork sausages, casing removed, cut into chunks
- 2 medium carrots, trimmed and cut into 1.5cm pieces
- 1 medium celery stalk, trimmed and cut into 1.5cm pieces

- 2 small onions, quartered
- 1 tbsp olive oil
- 1/2 tsp hot paprika
- 1 tsp garlic granules
- 1 tsp mustard powder
- Sea salt and ground black pepper, to taste

Instructions

1. Toss the vegetables with olive oil and spices until they are well coated on all sides.
2. Place the sausages in the zone 1 drawer (with a lightly greased crisper plate).
3. Arrange the vegetable in a lightly greased roasting tin; add the roasting tin to the zone 2 drawer (with no crisper plate inserted).
4. Select zone 1 and pair it with "AIR FRY" at 200°C for 15 minutes. Select zone 2 and pair it with "ROAST" at 190°C for 13 minutes. Select "SYNC" followed by the "START/STOP" button.
5. When zone 1 time reaches 8 minutes, turn the sausages over and spray them with nonstick cooking oil on the other side; reinsert the drawer to continue cooking.
6. When zone 2 time reaches 6 minutes, stir the vegetables and reinsert the drawer to continue cooking.
7. Top your vegetables with sausages and serve from the tin in the middle of the table. Bon appétit!

Per Serving:
Calories: 544g / Fat: 46.1g / Carbs: 11.5g / Fibre: 1.9g / Protein: 19.1g

Barbecued Pork Chops

Prep time: 5 minutes / Cook time: 16 minutes / Serves 4

Ingredients

- 1 kg good quality pork chops
- 2 tbsp soy sauce
- 1 tsp smoked paprika
- 2 tbsp tomato puree
- 1 tbsp dry sherry
- 1 thumb-sized piece ginger, grated

- 2 garlic cloves, crushed

Instructions

1. Insert crisper plates in both drawers. Spray the crisper plates with nonstick cooking oil.
2. Toss pork chops with the other Ingredients and lower them into the cooking basket.
3. Select zone 1 and pair it with "AIR FRY" at 200°C for 16 minutes. Select "MATCH" to duplicate settings across both zones. Press the "START/STOP" button.
4. At the halfway point, turn the pork chops over and reinsert the drawers to resume cooking.
5. Bon appétit

Per Serving:
Calories: 436g / Fat: 11.9g / Carbs: 4.4g / Fibre: 0.7g / Protein: 74.1g

Roast Loin of Pork with Herbs

Prep time: 10 minutes + marinating time / Cook time: 55 minutes / Serves 5

Ingredients

- 1kg loin of pork, skin scored, cut into two pieces
- 4 garlic cloves, crushed
- 100ml red wine
- 2 tbsp soy sauce
- 1 tsp dried rosemary
- 1 tsp dried parsley flakes
- 1 tbsp olive oil
- 1 tsp red pepper flakes, crushed
- Sea salt and ground black pepper, to taste

Instructions

1. Toss pork loin with the remaining ingredients. Leave the pork to marinate overnight in your fridge.
2. Remove the pork from the marinade and lower the pork pieces into the cooking basket.
3. Select zone 1 and pair it with "AIR FRY" at 195°C for 55 minutes. Select "MATCH" to duplicate settings across both zones. Press the "START/STOP" button.
4. At the halfway point, shake the basket, baste the pork with the reserved marinade, and

reinsert the drawers to resume cooking.

5.Bon appétit!

Per Serving:

Calories: 469g / Fat: 26.1g / Carbs: 3.5g / Fibre: 0.4g / Protein: 52.1g

Authentic Beef Stroganoff

Prep time: 10 minutes / Cook time: 26 minutes / Serves 5

Ingredients

- 2 tsp olive oil
- 1 large onion, chopped
- 250g mushrooms, sliced
- 600g fillet steak, sliced
- 1 tsp garlic paste
- Sea salt and ground black pepper, to taste
- 1 tsp cayenne pepper
- 1 (400g) can tomatoes, chopped
- 150g crème fraîche
- 2 tbsp fresh parsley, chopped

Instructions

1.Heat 1 teaspoon of olive oil in a frying pan over medium-high heat. Sauté the onion for about 3 minutes, until just tender.

2.Add the mushrooms and fillet steak, and continue to cook for 3 minutes.

3.Brush the inside of two oven-safe baking tins with the remaining 1 teaspoon of olive oil. Add the sauteed mixture along with the garlic paste, spices, and tomatoes to the baking tins; gently stir to combine and lower them into the drawers.

4.Select zone 1 and pair it with "AIR FRY" at 185°C for 20 minutes. Select "MATCH" to duplicate settings across both zones. Press the "START/STOP" button.

5.When zone 1 time reaches 10 minutes, gently stir the mixture and add the crème fraîche; reinsert the drawers to continue cooking.

6.Garnish Beef Stroganoff with fresh parsley.
  7.Devour!

Per Serving:

Calories: 311g / Fat: 13.8g / Carbs: 21.3g / Fibre: 2.4g / Protein: 27.9g

Pork and Green Bean Casserole

Prep time: 5 minutes / Cook time: 40 minutes / Serves 6

Ingredients

- 1 tbsp olive oil
- 100g bacon lardons
- 800g beef mince
- 100ml tomato puree
- 100ml hot water
- 1 tbsp beef bouillon granules
- 1 tsp paprika
- 1 medium onion, peeled and chopped
- 1 celery stalk, chopped
- 1 medium carrot, chopped
- 200g green beans
- 150g Parmesan cheese, preferably freshly grated

Instructions

1.Add all the ingredients, except the cheese, to a large bowl and stir until everything is well combined.

2.Spoon the mixture into two lightly greased baking tins. Add the baking tins to the drawers (without crisper plates).

3.Select zone 1 and pair it with "ROAST" at 180°C for 40 minutes. Select "MATCH" followed by the "START/STOP" button.

4.At the halfway point, gently stir the Ingredients using a wooden spoon. Top your casserole with Parmesan cheese and reinsert drawers to resume cooking.

5.Bon appétit!

Per Serving:

Calories: 511g / Fat: 30.9g / Carbs: 11.3g / Fibre: 2g / Protein: 46.1g

Cheesy Paprika Steak

Prep time: 1 hour / Cook time: 25 minutes / Serves 4

Ingredients

- 800g skirt steak, sliced
- 2 tbsp tamari sauce
- 100ml dry red wine

- 1 rosemary sprig, crushed
- 1 thyme sprig, crushed
- 2 garlic cloves, crushed
- Sea salt and ground black pepper, to taste
- 1 tsp paprika
- 2 tbsp tomato purée
- 1 tsp vegetable oil
- 100g blue cheese, crumbled

Instructions

1. In a ceramic bowl, place the steak, tamari sauce, wine, rosemary, thyme, garlic, salt, black pepper, paprika, and tomato purée. Leave to marinate for at least 1 hour.
2. Place skirt steaks in the cooking basket and brush them with vegetable oil.
3. Select zone 1 and pair it with "AIR FRY" at 200°C for 25 minutes. Select "MATCH" to duplicate settings across both zones. Press the "START/STOP" button.
4. At the halfway point, turn the steaks over and top them with blue cheese; reinsert the drawers to resume cooking.
5. Bon appétit!

Per Serving:
Calories: 391g / Fat: 20.5g / Carbs: 4.3g / Fibre: 0.8g / Protein: 47.4g

Chinese-Style Pork Medallions

Prep time: 5 minutes / Cook time: 18 minutes / Serves 4

Ingredients

- 1 kg pork medallions
- 2 tbsp soy sauce
- 2 tbsp honey
- 1 tsp smoked paprika
- 1 tbsp rice wine
- 1 thumb-sized piece of ginger, grated
- 2 garlic cloves, crushed

Instructions

1. Insert crisper plates in both drawers. Spray the crisper plates with nonstick cooking oil.
2. Toss pork medallions with the other Ingredients

and lower them into the cooking basket.
3. Select zone 1 and pair it with "AIR FRY" at 200°C for 18 minutes. Select "MATCH" to duplicate settings across both zones. Press the "START/STOP" button.
4. At the halfway point, turn the pork medallions over and reinsert the drawers to resume cooking.
5. Bon appétit

Per Serving:
Calories: 332g / Fat: 6.9g / Carbs: 11.5g / Fibre: 0.4g / Protein: 53.1g

Beef Sandwiches

Prep time: 10 minutes / Cook time: 20 minutes / Serves 6

Ingredients

- 600g sirloin steak, sliced
- 600g bell peppers, deseeded and halved
- 1 tbsp extra-virgin olive oil
- 2 garlic cloves, crushed
- Sea salt and ground black pepper, to taste
- 1 large tomato, diced
- 1 medium onion, sliced
- 6 sandwich rolls, split

Instructions

1. Toss the steak and bell peppers with olive oil, garlic, salt, and black pepper.
2. Place the steak in the zone 1 drawer and bell peppers in the zone 2 drawer.
3. Select zone 1 and pair it with "ROAST" at 195°C for 20 minutes. Select zone 2 and pair it with "ROAST" at 190°C for 10 minutes. Select "SYNC" followed by the "START/STOP" button.
4. At the half point, turn your Ingredients over to promote even cooking. Reinsert drawers to resume cooking.
5. Cut the steak into bite-sized strips. Assemble your sandwiches with sandwich rolls, tomato, and onion.
6. Bon appétit!

Per Serving:
Calories: 445g / Fat: 13.1g / Carbs: 56.1g / Fibre: 8.4g / Protein: 30.1g

CHAPTER 5 : FISH & SEAFOOD

Prawn & Cauliflower Salad

Prep time: 10 minutes / Cook time: 12 minutes / Serves 5

Ingredients
* 800g raw prawns, peeled, tails on
* 400g cauliflower florets, frozen and thawed
* Sea salt and ground black pepper, to taste
* 1 tsp Cajun seasoning mix
* 1 red onion, sliced
* 1 large tomato, diced
* 2 tbsp extra-virgin olive oil
* 1 tbsp fresh lemon juice

Instructions
1. Insert crisper plates in both drawers. Spray crisper plates with nonstick cooking oil.
2. Toss your prawns and cauliflower with 1 tablespoon of olive oil and spices.
3. Place your prawns in the zone 1 drawer and the cauliflower in the zone 2 drawer.
4. Select zone 1 and pair it with "AIR FRY" at 190°C for 8 minutes. Select zone 2 and pair it with "ROAST" at 200°C for 12 minutes. Select "SYNC" followed by the "START/STOP" button.
5. At the halfway point, stir your food to promote even cooking and reinsert the drawers to resume cooking.
6. Toss your prawns and cauliflower with the other Ingredients and serve immediately. Enjoy!

Per Serving:
Calories: 219g / Fat: 6.7g / Carbs: 6.9g / Fibre: 2.3g / Protein: 34.3g

BBQ Fish Tarts

Prep time: 10 minutes / Cook time: 12 minutes / Serves 8

Ingredients
* 350g sheets of filo pastry
* 200g codfish fillets, chopped
* 100ml BBQ sauce
* 50g cheddar cheese, crumbled
* 20g butter, melted

Instructions
1. Brush 8 muffin cases with cooking spray.
2. Completely thaw phyllo dough according to package directions. Pile up the filo pastry on a flat surface. Now, cut it into 8 squares and press them into the muffin cases.
3. In a mixing bowl, thoroughly combine the other ingredients. Divide the mixture between filo squares. Arrange the muffin cases in both drawers.
4. Select zone 1 and pair it with "BAKE" at 180°C for 12 minutes or until golden. Select "MATCH" followed by the "START/STOP" button.
5. Bon appétit!

Per Serving:
Calories: 275g / Fat: 6.5g / Carbs: 40.5g / Fibre: 1.6g / Protein: 12.4g

Restaurant-Style Fish Fillets

Prep time: 10 minutes / Cook time: 18 minutes / Serves 5

Ingredients
* 5 (200g each) tilapia fillets
* 1 large egg, beaten
* 150g plain flour
* Sea salt and ground black pepper, to taste
* 150g crushed crackers
* 1 tsp garlic granules
* 1 tsp dried parsley flakes
* 1 tbsp olive oil

Instructions
1. Pat the fish fillets dry with tea towels.
2. Create the breading station: Beat the egg until pale and frothy. In a separate shallow dish, mix the flour with salt and black pepper. Mix the crushed crackers, garlic granules and dried parsley in a third dish.
3. Coat the fish fillets in the flour. Dip fish fillets in the

beaten eggs; roll them over the cracker mixture.

4. Arrange the prepared fish fillets on the lightly greased crisper plates. Brush them with olive oil.

5. Select zone 1 and pair it with "AIR FRY" at 180°C for 18 minutes. Select "MATCH" to duplicate settings across both zones. Press the "START/STOP" button.

6. When zone 1 time reaches 9 minutes, turn the fish fillets over to promote even cooking. Reinsert the drawers to continue cooking.

7. Bon appétit!

Per Serving:
Calories: 422g / Fat: 22.4g / Carbs: 30.9g / Fibre: 1g / Protein: 26.6g

Seafood Jambalaya

Prep time: 5 minutes / Cook time: 20 minutes / Serves 6

Ingredients

- 300g long grain rice
- 400g frozen seafood mix, defrosted
- 1 celery stick, sliced
- 1 tbsp olive oil
- 1 large onion, sliced
- 2 garlic cloves, chopped
- 1 tbsp fresh thyme leaves
- 500ml hot fish stock
- 400g can chopped tomatoes
- 200g frozen peas

Instructions

1. Lightly grease two baking tins with cooking oil.

2. Cook the rice according to the pack Instructions; fluff the rice with a fork and divide it between the prepared baking tins.

3. Divide the other Ingredients between the prepared tins. Lower the tins into both drawers.

4. Select zone 1 and pair it with "AIR FRY" at 185°C for 20 minutes. Select "MATCH" to duplicate settings across both zones. Press the "START/STOP" button.

5. When zone 1 time reaches 10 minutes, gently stir the Ingredients to ensure even cooking.

Reinsert the drawers to continue cooking. Enjoy!

Per Serving:
Calories: 282g / Fat: 7.1g / Carbs: 38.1g / Fibre: 3.1g / Protein: 16g

Roast Fish Italian Style

Prep time: 10 minutes / Cook time: 20 minutes / Serves 4

Ingredients

- 4 (200g each) skinless pollock fillets
- 1 tbsp Italian spice mix
- 2 garlic cloves, peeled
- Sea salt and ground black pepper, to taste
- 2 tsp olive oil
- 400g new potatoes, scrubbed and cut into wedges
- 200g cherry tomatoes
- 1 small lemon, cut into wedges
- 1 tbsp fresh parsley leaves, chopped

Instructions

1. Pat fish fillets dry using tea towels. Coat fish fillets with spices, garlic, and 1 teaspoon of olive oil.

2. Toss new potatoes and cherry tomatoes with the remaining 1 teaspoon of olive oil, salt, and black pepper to taste.

3. Add pollock fillets to the zone 1 drawer and vegetables to the zone 2 drawer.

4. Select zone 1 and pair it with "ROAST" at 200°C for 12 minutes. Select zone 2 and pair it with "ROAST" at 190°C for 20 minutes. Select "SYNC" followed by the "START/STOP" button.

5. When zone 1 time reaches 6 minutes, turn the fish fillets over and reinsert the drawer to resume cooking.

6. When zone 2 time reaches 10 minutes, remove cherry tomatoes from the basket and toss the potatoes; reinsert the drawer to resume cooking.

7. On a serving platter, place fish fillets with potatoes, cherry tomatoes, and lemon wedges scattered over. Garnish with fresh parsley leaves and enjoy!

Per Serving:
Calories: 263g / Fat: 11.7g / Carbs: 30.5g / Fibre: 3.4g / Protein: 9.4g

Marinated Squid with Baby Carrots

Prep time: 1 hour / Cook time: 12 minutes / Serves 4

Ingredients
- 500g squid, tubes and tentacles
- 1 tbsp tamari sauce
- 100ml ale beer
- 1 tbsp yellow mustard
- Sea salt and ground black pepper, to your liking
- 100g corn flour
- 2 tsp olive oil
- 400g carrots, trimmed

Instructions
1. Insert crisper plates in both drawers and spray them with cooking oil.
2. Toss the squid with tamari sauce, beer, mustard, salt, and black pepper. Cover and let it marinate in your fridge for about 1 hour. Discard the marinade.
3. Coat the squid with the corn flour. Drizzle the squid with 1 teaspoon of olive oil.
4. Toss baby carrots with the remaining 1 teaspoon of olive oil, salt, and black pepper.
5. Add the squid to the zone 1 drawer and baby carrots the zone 2 drawer.
6. Select zone 1 and pair it with "AIR FRY" at 200°C for 12 minutes. Select zone 2 and pair it with "ROAST" at 200°C for 10 minutes. Select "SYNC" followed by the "START/STOP" button.
7. When zone 1 time reaches 6 minutes, turn the squid over and baste it with the reserved marinade; then, reinsert the drawer to resume cooking.
8. When zone 2 time reaches 10 minutes, toss baby carrots and reinsert the drawer to resume cooking.
9. Serve immediately and enjoy!

Per Serving:
Calories: 283g / Fat: 5g / Carbs: 33.4g / Fibre: 4.3g / Protein: 22.2g

Cheesy Halibut in a Parcel

Prep time: 10 minutes / Cook time: 15 minutes / Serves 4

Ingredients
- 2 garlic cloves, chopped
- 4 spring onions, chopped
- 4 (150g each) halibut fillets
- 2 tbsp dry sherry wine
- 2 tsp olive oil
- 2 tbsp soy sauce
- 1 tsp red pepper flakes
- Sea salt and ground black pepper, to taste
- 100g parmesan cheese, grated

Instructions
1. Cut out 4 squares of greaseproof paper, using scissors (each about 30cm).
2. Divide garlic and spring onions between greaseproof paper pieces. Top them with halibut fillets and drizzle everything with wine, olive oil, and soy sauce. Season them with red pepper flakes, salt, and black pepper
3. Then, fold over the edges of the foil to seal. Lay the halibut parcels onto the crisper plates.
4. Select zone 1 and pair it with "AIR FRY" at 200°C for 15 minutes. Select "MATCH" to duplicate settings across both zones. Press the "START/STOP" button.
5. When zone 1 time reaches 8 minutes, open the greaseproof paper pieces and top your fish with cheese. Reinsert the drawers to continue cooking.
6. Bon appétit!

Per Serving:
Calories: 301g / Fat: 11.7g / Carbs: 2.2g / Fibre: 0.4g / Protein: 44.3g

Spicy Sea Scallops with Roasted Leeks

Prep time: 10 minutes / Cook time: 12 minutes / Serves 4

Ingredients
- 600g sea scallops
- 1 tsp fennel seeds

- 1 large garlic clove, peeled
- 1 rosemary sprig, leaves picked
- Sea salt and ground black pepper, to taste
- 1 medium lemon, freshly squeezed
- 2 tbsp extra-virgin olive oil
- 600g leeks, quartered

Instructions

1. Insert crisper plates in both drawers and spray them with cooking oil.
2. Toss the scallops and leeks with the remaining ingredients.
3. Add the scallops to the zone 1 drawer and the leeks to the zone 2 drawer.
4. Select zone 1 and pair it with "AIR FRY" at 200°C for 12 minutes. Select zone 2 and pair it with "AIR FRY" at 190°C for 12 minutes. Select "SYNC" followed by the "START/STOP" button.
5. Shake the drawers halfway through the cooking time to ensure even cooking. Enjoy!

Per Serving:

Calories: 284g / Fat: 8.6g / Carbs: 24.8g / Fibre: 2.7g / Protein: 27.4g

Seafood Quinoa Pilau

Prep time: 5 minutes / Cook time: 20 minutes / Serves 5

Ingredients

- 200g quinoa, rinsed and drained
- 500g frozen seafood mix, defrosted
- 1 tbsp olive oil
- 1 large onion, sliced
- 2 garlic cloves, chopped
- 1L hot fish stock
- 200g frozen peas

Instructions

1. Spray two baking tins with cooking oil. Mix all the Ingredients until everything is well incorporated.
2. Divide the mixture between the prepared tins. Lower the tins into both drawers.
3. Select zone 1 and pair it with "AIR FRY" at 180°C for 20 minutes. Select "MATCH" to duplicate settings across both zones. Press the "START/STOP" button.
4. When zone 1 time reaches 9 minutes, gently stir the Ingredients to ensure even cooking. Reinsert the drawers to continue cooking.
5. Devour!

Per Serving:

Calories: 292g / Fat: 6.2g / Carbs: 33.6g / Fibre: 5g / Protein: 22.2g

Shrimp Tacos

Prep time: 10 minutes / Cook time: 15 minutes / Serves 4

Ingredients

- 500g shrimp
- 4 bell peppers, deseeded and halved
- 1 tbsp olive oil
- 1 tsp taco spice mix
- Sea salt and ground black pepper, to taste
- 1 small onion, sliced
- 100ml salsa
- 4 tortillas

Instructions

1. Toss the shrimp and peppers with olive oil and spices. Add the shrimp to the zone 1 drawer and bell peppers to the zone 2 drawer.
2. Select zone 1 and pair it with "AIR FRYER" at 200°C for 12 minutes. Select zone 2 and pair it with "ROAST" at 180°C for 15 minutes. Select "SYNC" followed by the "START/STOP" button.
3. At the halfway point, turn the shrimp and peppers over and reinsert the drawers to resume cooking; cut the peppers into strips.
4. Pile air-fried shrimp into tortillas along with roasted peppers, onions, and salsa. Enjoy!

Per Serving:

Calories: 344g / Fat: 9g / Carbs: 30.6g / Fibre: 14g / Protein: 34.6g

Zesty Shrimp with Courgette

Prep time: 10 minutes / Cook time: 12 minutes / Serves 4

Ingredients

- 600g shrimp
- 2 garlic cloves, crushed
- 1 rosemary sprig, leaves picked and chopped
- 1 tsp cayenne pepper
- Sea salt and ground black pepper, to taste
- 1 medium lemon, freshly squeezed
- 2 tbsp extra-virgin olive oil
- 600g courgettes, deseeded and halved

Instructions

1. Insert crisper plates in both drawers and spray them with cooking oil.
2. Toss the shrimp and courgettes with the remaining ingredients.
3. Add the shrimp to the zone 1 drawer and the courgettes to the zone 2 drawer.
4. Select zone 1 and pair it with "AIR FRY" at 200°C for 12 minutes. Select zone 2 and pair it with "AIR FRY" at 200°C for 8 minutes. Select "SYNC" followed by the "START/STOP" button.
5. Shake the drawers halfway through the cooking time to ensure even cooking. Enjoy!

Per Serving:
Calories: 264g / Fat: 9g / Carbs: 7.3g / Fibre: 1.7g / Protein: 36g

Indian Fish Mappas

Prep time: 5 minutes / Cook time: 25 minutes / Serves 6

Ingredients

- 2 tsp coconut oil, melted
- 400g pollock fillets, sliced
- 1 celery stick, sliced
- 1 tbsp olive oil
- 1 large onion, sliced
- 2 garlic cloves, chopped
- 1 chilli pepper
- 5-6 curry leave
- 1 tbsp fresh thyme leaves
- 200g basmati rice
- 450g tomatoes, cut into chunks
- 2 tbsp tikka curry paste

- 400g can of coconut milk

Instructions

1. Lightly grease two baking trays with cooking oil.
2. Divide the Ingredients between the prepared trays. Lower the trays into both drawers.
3. Select zone 1 and pair it with "AIR FRY" at 185°C for 25 minutes. Select "MATCH" to duplicate settings across both zones. Press the "START/STOP" button.
4. When zone 1 time reaches 10 minutes, add the coconut milk, stir to combine, and reinsert the drawers to continue cooking. Enjoy!

Per Serving:
Calories: 574g / Fat: 38.2g / Carbs: 46.4g / Fibre: 3g / Protein: 15.1g

Prawn and Tomato Sandwich

Prep time: 10 minutes / Cook time: 15 minutes / Serves 4

Ingredients

- 400g raw king prawns, peeled
- Sea salt and ground black pepper, to taste
- 1 tsp cayenne pepper
- 1 tsp dried parsley flakes
- 2 tsp olive oil
- 1 large egg, beaten
- 100g cornflakes, crushed
- 400g cherry tomatoes, trimmed and cut into chips
- 1 large baguette, cut into 4 pieces

Instructions

1. Insert a crisper plate in the zone 1 drawer. Spray the crisper plate with nonstick cooking oil.
2. Toss king prawns with spices and 1 teaspoon of olive oil. Toss cherry tomatoes with the remaining 1 teaspoon of olive oil, salt, and black pepper.
3. In a shallow bowl, whisk the egg and then, dip your prawns into the egg. After that, roll them over the crushed cornflakes.
4. Place your prawns in the zone 1 drawer and cherry tomatoes in the zone 2 drawer.

5. Select zone 1 and pair it with "AIR FRY" at 200°C for 15 minutes. Select zone 2 and pair it with "ROAST" at 180°C for 15 minutes. Select "SYNC" followed by the "START/STOP" button.
6. At the halfway point, shake the basket to promote even cooking; reinsert the drawers to resume cooking.
7. Assemble your sandwiches with fried prawns and cherry tomatoes; add toppings of choice and enjoy!

Per Serving:
Calories: 497g / Fat: 8g / Carbs: 75g / Fibre: 5.9g / Protein: 32.1g

Baked Avocado Eggs with Shrimp

Prep time: 10 minutes / Cook time: 11 minutes / Serves 6

Ingredients
* 3 large avocados, pitted and cut in half
* 6 small eggs
* Sea salt and ground black pepper, to taste
* 1/2 tsp garlic granules
* 200g shrimp, chopped
* 120g cheddar cheese, crumbled

Instructions
1. Cut the avocados in half and carefully remove the pits. Scoop out about 2 tablespoons of avocado flesh from the centre of each half and set it aside.
2. Whisk the eggs with the reserved avocado flesh. Spoon the mixture into each avocado cup. Season with salt, black pepper, and garlic granules.
3. After that, top the eggs with chopped shrimp and add avocado halves to both drawers.
4. Select zone 1 and pair it with "BAKE" at 200°C for 11 minutes. Select "MATCH" followed by the "START/STOP" button.
5. At the halfway point, top avocado eggs with cheese. Reinsert drawers to resume cooking. Enjoy!

Per Serving:
Calories: 288g / Fat: 20.3g / Carbs: 11.7g / Fibre: 6.9g / Protein: 16.3g

Tuna Steak with Broccoli

Prep time: 10 minutes / Cook time: 12 minutes / Serves 4

Ingredients
* 800g tuna steaks
* 1 tsp hot paprika
* 1 tsp dried oregano
* 1 tsp dried parsley flakes
* 1 tsp garlic granules
* Sea salt and ground black pepper, to taste
* 400g broccoli florets
* 2 tsp olive oil
* 1 tbsp fresh lime juice

Instructions
1. Insert crisper plates in both drawers. Spray crisper plates with nonstick cooking oil.
2. Toss tuna steaks with spices, 1 teaspoon of olive oil, and lemon juice. Toss broccoli florets with the remaining 1 teaspoon of olive oil, salt, and black pepper.
3. Place tuna steaks in the zone 1 drawer and the broccoli florets in the zone 2 drawer.
4. Select zone 1 and pair it with "AIR FRY" at 200°C for 12 minutes. Select zone 2 and pair it with "ROAST" at 200°C for 10 minutes. Select "SYNC" followed by the "START/STOP" button.
5. At the halfway point, toss your food to promote even cooking; reinsert the drawers to resume cooking.
6. Serve immediately and enjoy!

Per Serving:
Calories: 269g / Fat: 4.7g / Carbs: 8.7g / Fibre: 3.1g / Protein: 47.2g

Seafood Conge

Prep time: 5 minutes / Cook time: 20 minutes / Serves 4

Ingredients
* 200g white rice
* 200g frozen shrimp
* 200g frozen crab sticks

- 1 tbsp olive oil
- 1 large onion, sliced
- 2 garlic cloves, chopped
- 1 tablespoon Shaoxing wine
- 400g can chopped tomatoes with garlic
- 300ml chicken bone broth

Instructions

1. Spray two baking tins with cooking oil.
2. Cook the rice according to the pack Instructions; fluff the rice with a fork and divide it between the prepared baking tins.
3. Divide the other Ingredients between the prepared tins. Stir to combine well and lower the tins into both drawers.
4. Select zone 1 and pair it with "AIR FRY" at 180°C for 20 minutes. Select "MATCH" to duplicate settings across both zones. Press the "START/STOP" button.
5. When zone 1 time reaches 10 minutes, gently stir the Ingredients and reinsert the drawers to continue cooking. Enjoy!

Per Serving:
Calories: 414g / Fat: 5.1g / Carbs: 64.1g / Fibre: 6.2g / Protein: 29.8g

Mediterranean-Style Roast Fish

Prep time: 10 minutes / Cook time: 25 minutes / Serves 4

Ingredients
- 800g sea bass fillets
- 1 tbsp dried oregano
- 1 tsp dried basil
- 1 tsp dried rosemary
- 2 tbsp lemon juice
- 2 tsp olive oil
- 400g Maris Piper potatoes, peeled and cut into wedges
- Sea salt and ground black pepper, to taste

Instructions

1. Pat sea bass dry using tea towels. Toss sea bass with spices, lemon juice, and 1 teaspoon of olive oil.
2. Toss potatoes with the remaining 1 teaspoon of

olive oil, salt, and pepper.
3. Add sea bass to the zone 1 drawer and potatoes to the zone 2 drawer.
4. Select zone 1 and pair it with "ROAST" at 200°C for 12 minutes. Select zone 2 and pair it with "ROAST" at 200°C for 25 minutes. Select "SYNC" followed by the "START/STOP" button.
5. When zone 1 time reaches 6 minutes, turn the fish over using silicone-tipped tongs. Reinsert the drawer to continue cooking.
6. When zone 2 time reaches 12 minutes, turn the potatoes over using silicone-tipped tongs. Reinsert the drawer to continue cooking.
7. Bon appétit!

Per Serving:
Calories: 298g / Fat: 6.4g / Carbs: 19.2g / Fibre: 2.6g / Protein: 39.2g

Sea Scallops with Mushrooms

Prep time: 10 minutes / Cook time: 12 minutes / Serves 4

Ingredients
- 400g sea scallops, cleaned
- 1 tsp garlic granules
- 1 tsp dried basil
- 1 tsp mustard powder
- Sea salt and ground black pepper, to taste
- 300g button mushrooms
- 1 medium lemon, juiced
- 2 tsp olive oil

Instructions

1. Toss your scallops and mushrooms with the other ingredients. Add sea scallops to the zone 1 drawer (with a crisper plate).
2. Add mushrooms to the zone 2 drawer (without a crisper plate).
3. Select zone 1 and pair it with "AIR FRY" at 200°C for 8 minutes. Select zone 2 and pair it with "ROAST" at 185°C for 12 minutes. Select "SYNC" followed by the "START/STOP" button.
4. When zone 1 time reaches 4 minutes, turn the scallops over using silicone-tipped tongs. Reinsert the drawer to continue cooking.

5. When zone 2 time reaches 6 minutes, shake the drawer for a few seconds to promote even cooking. Reinsert the drawer to continue cooking. Enjoy!

Per Serving:

Calories: 169g / Fat: 3.6g / Carbs: 12g / Fibre: 1.8g / Protein: 23.1g

Garlicky Halibut Steak with Asparagus

Prep time: 10 minutes / Cook time: 12 minutes / Serves 4

Ingredients

* 800g halibut steaks
* 1 tbsp Italian spice mix
* 2 garlic cloves, crushed
* Sea salt and ground black pepper, to taste
* 400g asparagus spears, trimmed
* 2 tsp olive oil
* 1 tbsp fresh lime juice

Instructions

1. Insert crisper plates in both drawers. Spray crisper plates with nonstick cooking oil.
2. Toss halibut steaks with spices, garlic, 1 teaspoon of olive oil, and lemon juice. Toss asparagus with the remaining 1 teaspoon of olive oil, salt, and black pepper.
3. Place halibut steaks in the zone 1 drawer and the asparagus in the zone 2 drawer.
4. Select zone 1 and pair it with "AIR FRY" at 200°C for 12 minutes. Select zone 2 and pair it with "ROAST" at 200°C for 10 minutes. Select "SYNC" followed by the "START/STOP" button.
5. At the halfway point, toss your food to promote even cooking; reinsert the drawers to resume cooking.
6. Bon appétit!

Per Serving:

Calories: 233g / Fat: 5g / Carbs: 5.7g / Fibre: 2.3g / Protein: 39.6g

Roast Fish with Chorizo

Prep time: 10 minutes / Cook time: 20 minutes / Serves 4

Ingredients

* 600g small sea bass
* 1 tbsp Spanish paprika
* Sea salt and ground black pepper, to taste
* 2 garlic cloves, peeled
* 2 tsp olive oil
* 200g chorizo, skin removed and sliced
* 400g potatoes, peeled and cut into wedges

Instructions

1. Pat fish fillets dry using tea towels. Coat fish fillets with spices, garlic, and 1 teaspoon of olive oil.
2. Toss new potatoes with the remaining 1 teaspoon of olive oil, salt, and black pepper to taste.
3. Add the fish to the zone 1 drawer; add potatoes and chorizo to the zone 2 drawer.
4. Select zone 1 and pair it with "ROAST" at 200°C for 12 minutes. Select zone 2 and pair it with "ROAST" at 190°C for 20 minutes. Select "SYNC" followed by the "START/STOP" button.
5. When zone 1 time reaches 6 minutes, turn the fish fillets over and reinsert the drawer to resume cooking.
6. When zone 2 time reaches 10 minutes, remove the chorizo from the basket and toss the potatoes; reinsert the drawer to resume cooking.
7. Bon appétit!

Per Serving:

Calories: 481g / Fat: 24.7g / Carbs: 20.9g / Fibre: 3g / Protein: 42.2g

Garlicky Prawns with Roasted Peppers

Prep time: 10 minutes / Cook time: 12 minutes / Serves 4

Ingredients

* 600g prawns
* 2 garlic cloves, crushed
* 1 rosemary sprig, leaves picked and chopped
* 1 tsp cayenne pepper
* Sea salt and ground black pepper, to taste
* 1 medium lemon, freshly squeezed
* 2 tbsp extra-virgin olive oil
* 600g bell peppers, deseeded and halved

Instructions

1. Insert crisper plates in both drawers and spray them with cooking oil.
2. Toss the prawns and peppers with the remaining ingredients.
3. Add the prawns to the zone 1 drawer and the peppers to the zone 2 drawer.
4. Select zone 1 and pair it with "AIR FRY" at 200°C for 12 minutes. Select zone 2 and pair it with "AIR FRY" at 190°C for 10 minutes. Select "SYNC" followed by the "START/STOP" button.
5. Shake the drawers halfway through the cooking time to ensure even cooking. Enjoy!

Per Serving:

Calories: 225g / Fat: 4.2g / Carbs: 16.9g / Fibre: 3g / Protein: 33.5g

Spanish Paella

Prep time: 5 minutes / Cook time: 20 minutes / Serves 4

Ingredients

* 200g paella or risotto rice
* 400g frozen seafood mix, defrosted
* 1 tbsp olive oil
* 1 large onion, sliced
* 2 garlic cloves, chopped
* 300ml chicken stock
* 400g can chopped tomatoes with garlic
* 3 tbsp dry sherry wine
* 100g pack of chorizo sausage, chopped

Instructions

1. Spray two baking tins with cooking oil.
2. Cook the rice according to the pack Instructions; fluff the rice with a fork and divide it between the prepared baking tins.
3. Divide the other Ingredients between the prepared tins. Stir to combine well and lower the tins into both drawers.
4. Select zone 1 and pair it with "AIR FRY" at 180°C for 20 minutes. Select "MATCH" to duplicate settings across both zones. Press the "START/STOP" button.

5. When zone 1 time reaches 10 minutes, gently stir the Ingredients and reinsert the drawers to continue cooking. Enjoy!

Per Serving:

Calories: 461g / Fat: 1.9g / Carbs: 79g / Fibre: 6.3g / Protein: 11.5g

Herb-crusted fish Fillets

Prep time: 10 minutes / Cook time: 20 minutes / Serves 4

Ingredients

* 4 (200g each) codfish fillets
* 1 large egg, beaten
* 150g plain flour
* 150g fresh breadcrumbs
* 1 tbsp fresh parsley, chopped
* 1 tbsp fresh cilantro, chopped
* 1 tbsp rosemary, chopped
* Sea salt and ground black pepper, to taste
* 1 tbsp olive oil

Instructions

1. Pat the codfish fillets dry with tea towels.
2. Create the breading station: Beat the egg until pale and frothy. In a separate shallow dish, place the flour. Mix the breadcrumbs with the herbs, salt, and pepper in a third dish.
3. Coat the fish fillets in the flour. Dip fish fillets in the beaten eggs; roll them over the breadcrumb mixture.
4. Arrange the prepared fish fillets on the lightly greased crisper plates. Brush them with olive oil.
5. Select zone 1 and pair it with "AIR FRY" at 185°C for 20 minutes. Select "MATCH" to duplicate settings across both zones. Press the "START/STOP" button.
6. When zone 1 time reaches 9 minutes, turn the fish fillets over to promote even cooking. Reinsert the drawers to continue cooking.
7. Bon appétit!

Per Serving:

Calories: 471g / Fat: 16.8g / Carbs: 48.5g / Fibre: 2.3g / Protein: 29.5g

CHAPTER 6: HEALTHY VEGETARIAN & VEGAN

Vegan Wraps with Aubergine and Mushrooms

Prep time: 10 minutes / Cook time: 16 minutes / Serves 4

Ingredients

* 500g aubergine, peeled and sliced
* 500g brown mushrooms, halved
* 1 tsp paprika
* 1 tsp garlic granules
* Sea salt and ground black pepper, to taste
* 2 tsp olive oil
* 4 large tortillas
* 4 tbsp hummus

Instructions

1. Insert the crisper plates in both drawers and spray them with cooking oil.
2. Toss the aubergine slices with spices and 1 teaspoon of olive oil; arrange them in the zone 1 drawer.
3. Drizzle your mushrooms with the remaining 1 teaspoon of olive oil, salt, and pepper; place it in the zone 2 drawer.
4. Select zone 1 and pair it with "ROAST" at 200°C for 10 minutes. Select zone 2 and pair it with "AIR FRY" at 180°C for 10 minutes. Select "SYNC" followed by the "START/STOP" button.
5. When zone 1 time reaches 5 minutes, toss the drawer to ensure even cooking; reinsert the drawer to resume cooking.
6. When zone 2 time reaches 5 minutes, shake the drawer and reinsert it to resume cooking.
7. Assemble vegan wraps with tortillas, roasted aubergine slices, mushrooms, and hummus; roll them up.
8. Use "REHEAT" mode to bake your wraps at 180°C for 6 minutes, until warmed through.
9. Bon appétit!

Per Serving:
Calories: 444g / Fat: 10.8g / Carbs: 74.2g / Fibre: 5.3g / Protein: 14.3g

Spicy Broccoli Croquettes

Prep time: 10 minutes / Cook time: 20 minutes / Serves 6

Ingredients

* 500g small broccoli florets
* 1 (400g) cans of red kidney beans, rinsed drained and mashed
* 1 small onion, peeled
* 2 garlic cloves, peeled
* 1 chilli pepper, deseeded and minced
* 100g rolled oats
* 1/2 tsp ground cumin
* Sea salt and ground black pepper, to taste
* 1 tbsp olive oil

Instructions

1. Insert the crisper plates in both drawers and spray them with cooking oil.
2. Add all the Ingredients to a bowl of your food processor. Blend the Ingredients until everything is well incorporated.
3. Shape the mixture into equal patties and arrange them on the crisper plates.
4. Select zone 1 and pair it with "AIR FRY" at 180°C for 20 minutes. Select "MATCH" to duplicate settings across both zones. Press the "START/STOP" button.
5. When zone 1 time reaches 10 minutes, turn the croquettes over and spray them with cooking oil on the other side; reinsert the drawers to continue cooking.
6. Bon appétit!

Per Serving:
Calories: 214g / Fat: 4.2g / Carbs: 34.7g / Fibre: 9.3g / Protein: 11.3g

Baked Sweet Potatoes with Black Beans

Prep time: 10 minutes / Cook time: 40 minutes / Serves 4

Ingredients

* 4 (220-240g each) sweet potatoes

- 2 tbsp olive oil
- 200g mushrooms, sliced
- 2 medium onions, quartered
- 1 tsp red pepper flakes
- Sea salt and ground black pepper, to taste
- 200g canned or cooked black beans, drained and rinsed
- 8 black olives, pitted and halved
- 4 sun-dried tomatoes in oil, chopped

Instructions

1. Pierce sweet potatoes with a fork a few times and drizzle them with 1 tablespoon of olive oil. Place sweet potatoes in the zone 1 drawer.
2. Toss the mushrooms and onions with spices and the remaining 1 tablespoon of olive oil. Arrange your vegetables in the zone 2 drawer.
3. Select zone 1 and pair it with "ROAST" at 180°C for 40 minutes. Select zone 2 and pair it with "AIR FRY" at 185°C for 10 minutes. Select "SYNC" followed by the "START/STOP" button.
4. When zone 1 time reaches 20 minutes, split the potatoes down the middle; reinsert the drawer to resume cooking.
5. When zone 2 time reaches 5 minutes, shake the cooking basket to promote even cooking; reinsert the drawer to resume cooking.
6. Cut the vegetables into chunks. Mix the vegetables, black beans, and dried tomatoes; divide the mixture between warm potatoes. Enjoy!

Per Serving:
Calories: 474g / Fat: 9.3g / Carbs: 90.2g / Fibre: 14.3g / Protein: 14.4g

Peppers with Halloumi and Marinated Mushrooms

Prep time: 5 minutes / Cook time: 23 minutes / Serves 4

Ingredients

- 8 small peppers, deveined
- 250g jar antipasti marinated mushrooms
- 100g cooked brown rice
- 200g halloumi cheese, crumbled
- 2 tsp chopped fresh parsley

- 1 tsp Italian spice mix
- Sea salt and ground black pepper, to taste

Instructions

1. Spray the peppers with nonstick cooking oil and place them in both drawers.
2. Select zone 1 and pair it with "ROAST" at 180°C for 10 minutes. Select "MATCH" to duplicate settings across both zones. Press the "START/STOP" button.
3. In a mixing bowl, thoroughly combine the other ingredients. Divide the mixture between bell peppers and arrange the peppers in baking tins. Lower the tins into the cooking basket of your Ninja Foodi.
4. Select zone 1 and pair it with "BAKE" at 185°C for 13 minutes. Select "MATCH" to duplicate settings across both zones. Press the "START/STOP" button.
5. Bon appétit!

Per Serving:
Calories: 244g / Fat: 11.3g / Carbs: 27.1g / Fibre: 4.4g / Protein: 11.3g

Roasted Peppers with Tofu

Prep time: 10 minutes / Cook time: 12 minutes / Serves 4

Ingredients

- 400g bell peppers, deseeded and halved
- 400g tofu, pressed and sliced
- 1 tsp garlic granules
- 1/2 tsp cumin powder
- 2 tsp olive oil
- 1 tbsp soy sauce

Instructions

1. Toss bell peppers and tofu with spices, olive oil, and soy sauce.
2. Arrange bell peppers in the zone 1 drawer and tofu in the zone 2 drawer.
3. Select zone 1 and pair it with "ROAST" at 190°C for 12 minutes. Select zone 2 and pair it with "ROAST" at 180°C for 10 minutes. Select "SYNC" followed by the "START/STOP" button.
4. When zone 1 time reaches 6 minutes, toss the

drawer to ensure even cooking; reinsert the drawer to resume cooking.

5. When zone 2 time reaches 5 minutes, shake the drawer and reinsert it to resume cooking.

6. Bon appétit!

Per Serving:

Calories: 333g / Fat: 23.4g / Carbs: 18.1g / Fibre: 4.9g / Protein: 18.5g

Stuffed Peppers with Red Lentils

Prep time: 5 minutes / Cook time: 23 minutes / Serves 5

Ingredients

- 5 medium peppers, deveined
- 200g canned or cooked red lentils, drained
- 200g rice, cooked • 50ml tomato paste
- 1 tsp Italian spice mix
- Sea salt and ground black pepper, to taste
- 100g tofu, crumbled

Instructions

1. Spray the peppers with nonstick cooking oil and place them in both drawers.

2. Select zone 1 and pair it with "ROAST" at 180°C for 10 minutes. Select "MATCH" to duplicate settings across both zones. Press the "START/STOP" button.

3. In a mixing bowl, thoroughly combine the other ingredients. Divide the mixture between bell peppers and arrange the peppers in two baking trays.

4. Lower the trays into both drawers.

5. Select zone 1 and pair it with "ROAST" at 190°C for 13 minutes. Select "MATCH" to duplicate settings across both zones. Press the "START/STOP" button.

6. Bon appétit!

Per Serving:

Calories: 299g / Fat: 4.8g / Carbs: 52.7g / Fibre: 8.1g / Protein: 11.6g

Coconut Quinoa Bake

Prep time: 10 minutes / Cook time: 27 minutes / Serves 6

Ingredients

- 2 tsp coconut oil, melted

- 250g quinoa, rinsed
- 1l coconut milk
- 50g coconut shreds • 50g almonds, slivered
- 100g golden raisins
- 1/2 vanilla bean • 1 cinnamon stick
- A pinch of sea salt
- A pinch of grated nutmeg

Instructions

1. Brush the inside of two baking trays with the melted coconut oil.

2. Tip the quinoa into a deep saucepan and pour in the milk; bring it to a boil. Reduce the heat to medium-low and leave to simmer for approximately 15 minutes, stirring continuously, until the millet is tender.

3. Mix the quinoa with the other Ingredients and spoon the mixture into two baking tins. Add the baking tins to the drawers.

4. Select zone 1 and pair it with "BAKE" at 180°C for 12 minutes. Select "MATCH" to duplicate settings across both zones. Press the "START/STOP" button.

5. Bon appétit!

Per Serving:

Calories: 350g / Fat: 11.5g / Carbs: 50g / Fibre: 4.7g / Protein: 13.7g

Stuffed Tomatoes with Chestnut Mushrooms

Prep time: 10 minutes / Cook time: 13 minutes / Serves 6

Ingredients

- 6 medium tomatoes, deseeded and halved
- 1 small courgette, chopped
- 100g chestnut mushrooms, wiped and sliced
- 400g tofu, pressed and sliced
- 1 tsp garlic granules
- 1/2 tsp cumin powder
- 2 tsp olive oil
- 1 tbsp soy sauce

Instructions

1. Pat tomatoes dry with tea towels.

2. In a mixing bowl, thoroughly combine the other

ingredients. Divide the mixture between your tomatoes and arrange the tomatoes in two baking trays.

3. Lower the trays into both drawers.
4. Select zone 1 and pair it with "ROAST" at 190°C for 13 minutes. Select "MATCH" to duplicate settings across both zones. Press the "START/STOP" button.
5. Bon appétit!

Per Serving:

Calories: 323g / Fat: 22.5g / Carbs: 17.5g / Fibre: 5.7g / Protein: 19.2g

Cauliflower Crust Pan Pizza

Prep time: 10 minutes / Cook time: 15 minutes / Serves 4

Ingredients

- 600g raw cauliflower
- 3 large eggs
- 200g mozzarella cheese, shredded
- 1 tbsp olive oil
- Sea salt and freshly ground black pepper, to taste
- 1 tsp Italian spice mix
- 200ml pizza sauce
- 200g mushrooms, sliced

Instructions

1. Grate your cauliflower using a box grater or food processor.
2. Now, sauté the cauliflower rice in a frying pan on medium heat for about 5 minutes. Drain and reserve.
3. Place the drained cauliflower rice in a large mixing bowl. Fold in the eggs, cheese, olive oil, and spices; mix everything to form the pizza dough.
4. Press two pizza crusts into 2 parchment-lined baking trays. Top them with pizza sauce and mushrooms.
5. Select zone 1 and pair it with "BAKE" at 200°C for 10 minutes. Select "MATCH" to duplicate settings across both zones. Press the "START/STOP" button.
6. Bon appétit!

Per Serving:

Calories: 220g / Fat: 7.6g / Carbs: 14.8g / Fibre: 5.3g / Protein: 25.2g

Apple Pancakes

Prep time: 10 minutes / Cook time: 20 minutes / Serves 6

Ingredients

- 280g old-fashioned rolled oats
- 360g unsweetened applesauce
- 2 eggs
- 120ml almond milk
- 1 tsp vanilla extract
- 1 tsp pure maple syrup
- 2 tsp baking powder
- 1 tsp ground cinnamon
- A pinch of sea salt
- Olive oil, for cooking

Instructions

1. Begin by preheating your Ninja Dual Zone Air Fryer to 180°C. Now, brush two muffin tins with nonstick cooking spray.
2. In your food processor, mix all the Ingredients until everything is well incorporated.
3. Spoon the batter into the prepared muffin tins. Lower one muffin tin into each drawer.
4. Select zone 1 and pair it with "BAKE" at 180°C for 20 minutes. Select "MATCH" followed by the "START/STOP" button.
5. Transfer your pancakes to a cooling rack; let it stand for about 10 minutes before unmolding and serving.
6. Bon appétit!

Per Serving:

Calories: 266g / Fat: 6.9g / Carbs: 39.7g / Fibre: 5.5g / Protein: 11.6g

Courgette Lasagne

Prep time: 10 minutes / Cook time: 25 minutes / Serves 6

Ingredients

- Lasagne:
- 2 large courgettes
- 600g brown mushrooms, chopped
- 200ml vegetable broth
- 1 tsp dried oregano

- 1 tsp dried basil
- 1 tsp dried parsley flakes
- Sea salt and ground black pepper, to taste
- 400g can tomatoes
- 100g Parmesan cheese, grated
- Béchamel Sauce:
- 80g butter • 80g plain flour
- 1.5l milk
- Sea salt and ground black pepper, to taste
- A pinch of grated nutmeg

Instructions

1. Cut your courgettes into thin slices. Mix the other Ingredients for lasagne.
2. To make the béchamel sauce, melt the butter in a saucepan; then, cook the flour for 2 minutes, stirring continuously to avoid lumps.
3. Stir in the milk, a little at a time. Bring to a gentle simmer, whisking constantly. Season with salt, pepper, and nutmeg.
4. In two lightly greased baking trays, repeat the layers – zucchini slices, béchamel, mushroom filling, and parmesan cheese. Repeat until you run out of your ingredients.
5. Add the baking trays to the drawers (without crisper plates).
6. Select zone 1 and pair it with "BAKE" at 180°C for 20 minutes. Select "MATCH" followed by the "START/STOP" button. Bon appétit!

Per Serving:
Calories: 406g / Fat: 24.5g / Carbs: 30.3g / Fibre: 2.7g / Protein: 18.5g

Green Bean and Tofu Salad

Prep time: 10 minutes / Cook time: 10 minutes / Serves 4

Ingredients

- 400g green beans, trimmed
- 400g tofu, pressed and sliced
- 1 tsp garlic granules • 1/2 tsp onion powder
- 1 tsp dried oregano
- 1 tsp dried parsley flakes
- 2 tsp olive oil • 1 tbsp soy sauce
- 200g cherry tomatoes, halved
- 1 chilli pepper, sliced

- 1 small cucumber, sliced
- Dressing:
- 2 tbsp fresh lemon juice
- 1 tbsp extra-virgin olive oil
- 1 tsp garlic, crushed
- 1 tsp fresh ginger, peeled and grated

Instructions

1. Toss green beans and tofu with spices, olive oil, and soy sauce.
2. Arrange green beans in the zone 1 drawer and tofu in the zone 2 drawer.
3. Select zone 1 and pair it with "AIR FRY" at 200°C for 8 minutes. Select zone 2 and pair it with "ROAST" at 180°C for 10 minutes. Select "SYNC" followed by the "START/STOP" button.
4. When zone 1 time reaches 4 minutes, toss the drawer to ensure even cooking; reinsert the drawer to resume cooking.
5. When zone 2 time reaches 5 minutes, shake the drawer and reinsert it to resume cooking.
6. Meanwhile, make the dressing by whisking all the ingredients.
7. Assemble your salad with warm green beans, tofu, cherry tomatoes, chilli pepper, and cucumber. Dress your salad and serve immediately. Bon appétit!

Per Serving:
Calories: 332g / Fat: 13.2g / Carbs: 45.2g / Fibre: 13.7g / Protein: 18g

The Best Vegetarian Quiche Ever

Prep time: 10 minutes / Cook time: 25 minutes / Serves 4

Ingredients

- 400g brown mushrooms, chopped
- 200g tofu, crumbled
- 4 large eggs, beaten
- 100ml vegetable broth
- 1 medium bell pepper, deseeded and chopped
- 1 chilli pepper, deseeded and chopped
- 2 garlic cloves, minced
- 2 tbsp fresh parsley, chopped
- 1 tsp Italian spice mix
- Sea salt and ground black pepper, to taste

Instructions

1. Grease two baking trays with cooking oil.
2. In a mixing bowl, thoroughly combine all the ingredients. Divide the mixture between the prepared baking trays.
3. Lower them into the drawers (without crisper plates).
4. Select zone 1 and pair it with "BAKE" at 180°C for 25 minutes. Select "MATCH" followed by the "START/STOP" button.
5. Cut your quiche into wedges and serve immediately.
6. Bon appétit!

Per Serving:
Calories: 184g / Fat: 9.3g / Carbs: 10.9g / Fibre: 2.7g / Protein: 18g

Herb Potato Latkes

Prep time: 35 minutes / Cook time: 25 minutes / Serves 4

Ingredients

- 800g potatoes, grated
- 1 small onion, chopped
- 1 large egg, beaten
- 20g matzo meal
- 20g flat-leaf parsley, roughly chopped
- 20g coriander, roughly chopped
- 1 tsp paprika
- Sea salt and ground black pepper, to taste
- 1 tbsp olive oil

Instructions

1. Insert crisper plates in both drawers. Spray the crisper plates with nonstick cooking oil.
2. Use a food processor or a box grater to grate your potatoes; transfer them to a large bowl of very cold water. Let it sit for about 30 minutes.
3. Drain your potatoes and combine them with the remaining ingredients. Shape the mixture into small patties and arrange them in both drawers.
4. Select zone 1 and pair it with "AIR FRY" at 185°C for 25 minutes. Select "MATCH" followed by the "START/STOP" button.
5. When zone 1 time reaches 8 minutes, turn your latkes over and reinsert the drawers to resume cooking.
6. Bon appétit!

Per Serving:
Calories: 234g / Fat: 4.9g / Carbs: 42.4g / Fibre: 5.7g / Protein: 6.8g

Cauliflower & Buckwheat Burgers

Prep time: 10 minutes / Cook time: 20 minutes / Serves 4

Ingredients

- 500g small cauliflower florets
- 200g buckwheat, soaked overnight and rinsed
- 1 small onion, peeled
- 2 garlic cloves, peeled
- 1/2 tsp mustard powder
- 1/2 tsp ground cumin
- Sea salt and ground black pepper, to taste
- 1 tbsp olive oil

Instructions

1. Insert the crisper plates in both drawers and spray them with cooking oil.
2. Add all the Ingredients to a bowl of your food processor. Blend the Ingredients until everything is well incorporated.
3. Shape the mixture into equal patties and arrange them on the crisper plates.
4. Select zone 1 and pair it with "AIR FRY" at 180°C for 20 minutes. Select "MATCH" to duplicate settings across both zones. Press the "START/STOP" button.
5. When zone 1 time reaches 10 minutes, turn your burgers over and spray them with cooking oil on the other side; reinsert the drawers to continue cooking.
6. Bon appétit!

Per Serving:
Calories: 248g / Fat: 5.5g / Carbs: 45.3g / Fibre: 8.1g / Protein: 9.6g

Courgette and Black Bean Smothered Burritos

Prep time: 10 minutes / Cook time: 18 minutes / Serves 4

Ingredients

- 500g courgette, peeled and sliced
- 1 tsp paprika
- 1/2 tsp mustard powder
- 1 tsp garlic granules
- Sea salt and ground black pepper, to taste
- 1 tbsp olive oil
- 4 large tortillas
- 4 tbsp cheddar cheese, grated
- 4 tbsp sour cream
- 1 tbsp coriander, finely chopped

Instructions

1. Toss the courgette slices with spices and olive oil and arrange them in the cooking basket.
2. Select zone 1 and pair it with "AIR FRY" at 185°C for 12 minutes. Select "MATCH" to duplicate settings across both zones. Press the "START/STOP" button.
3. Assemble vegan wraps with tortillas, roasted courgette slices and cheese; wrap four burritos.
4. Mix the sour cream and coriander. Spread the sour cream mixture over your burritos.
5. Use "REHEAT" mode to bake your wraps at 180°C for 6 minutes, until warmed through.
6. Bon appétit!

Per Serving:
Calories: 434g / Fat: 12.5g / Carbs: 68g / Fibre: 4.1g / Protein: 12.4g

Mediterranean Stuffed Tomatoes

Prep time: 5 minutes / Cook time: 25 minutes / Serves 6

Ingredients

- 1 tbsp olive oil
- 6 large peppers, deveined
- 250g jar antipasti marinated mushrooms
- 100g cooked couscous
- 200g feta cheese, crumbled
- 1 tsp Mediterranean spice mix
- 12 Kalamata olives, pitted and sliced
- Sea salt and ground black pepper, to taste

Instructions

1. Brush the peppers with olive oil and place

them in both drawers.
2. Select zone 1 and pair it with "ROAST" at 180°C for 10 minutes. Select "MATCH" to duplicate settings across both zones. Press the "START/STOP" button.
3. In a mixing bowl, thoroughly combine the other ingredients. Divide the mixture between bell peppers and arrange the peppers in baking tins. Lower the tins into the cooking basket of your Ninja Foodi.
4. Select zone 1 and pair it with "BAKE" at 185°C for 15 minutes. Select "MATCH" to duplicate settings across both zones. Press the "START/STOP" button.
5. Bon appétit!

Per Serving:
Calories: 198g / Fat: 10.5g / Carbs: 17.7g / Fibre: 4.5g / Protein: 8.4g

Old-Fashioned Cauliflower Fritters

Prep time: 10 minutes / Cook time: 20 minutes / Serves 6

Ingredients

- 500g small cauliflower florets
- 1 small onion, peeled
- 2 garlic cloves, peeled
- 1 (400g) cans of pinto beans, rinsed drained and mashed
- 100g rolled oats
- 1/2 tsp mustard powder
- 1/2 tsp ground cumin
- Sea salt and ground black pepper, to taste
- 1 tbsp olive oil

Instructions

1. Insert the crisper plates in both drawers and spray them with cooking oil.
2. Add all the Ingredients to a bowl of your food processor. Blend the Ingredients until everything is well incorporated.
3. Shape the mixture into equal patties and arrange them on the crisper plates.
4. Select zone 1 and pair it with "AIR FRY" at 180°C for 20 minutes. Select "MATCH" to

duplicate settings across both zones. Press the "START/STOP" button.

5. When zone 1 time reaches 10 minutes, turn the patties over and spray them with cooking oil on the other side; reinsert the drawers to continue cooking.

6. Bon appétit!

Per Serving:

Calories: 178g / Fat: 4.1g / Carbs: 28.6g / Fibre: 7.2g / Protein: 8.2g

Portobello Mushrooms Fajitas

Prep time: 10 minutes / Cook time: 18 minutes / Serves 4

Ingredients

- 500g portobello mushrooms, sliced
- 2 large bell pepper, deseeded and halved
- 1 chilli pepper, deseeded and halved
- 1 medium onion, peeled and quartered
- 2 tbsp olive oil
- 1 tsp red pepper flakes
- Sea salt and freshly ground black pepper, to taste
- 1 tsp dried Mexican oregano
- 4 medium corn tortillas

Instructions

1. Insert crisper plates in both drawers. Spray the crisper plates with nonstick cooking oil.
2. Toss the mushrooms, peppers, and onions with olive oil and spices.
3. Place the mushrooms in the zone 1 drawer; place the peppers and onions in the zone 2 drawer.
4. Select zone 1 and pair it with "AIR FRY" at 185°C for 13 minutes. Select zone 2 and pair it with "ROAST" at 180°C for 15 minutes. Select "SYNC" followed by the "START/STOP" button.
5. Shake the basket once or twice to promote even cooking. Reinsert the drawers to resume cooking.
6. Add tortillas to both drawers. Select "REHEAT" at 170°C for 5 minutes.
7. Add the mushrooms to the warmed tortillas; top them with onions and peppers. Enjoy!

Per Serving:

Calories: 324g / Fat: 11.5g / Carbs: 46.9g / Fibre: 11.5g / Protein: 10.6g

Vegan Mushroom & Courgette Casserole

Prep time: 10 minutes / Cook time: 20 minutes / Serves 4

Ingredients

- 400g courgette, sliced
- 400g brown mushrooms, chopped
- 400g tofu, crumbled
- 200ml tomato sauce
- 1 shallot, sliced
- 1 medium bell pepper, deseeded and chopped
- 2 garlic cloves, minced
- 2 tbsp fresh parsley, chopped
- 1 tbsp olive oil
- Sea salt and ground black pepper, to taste

Instructions

1. Grease two baking trays with cooking oil.
2. In a mixing bowl, thoroughly combine all the ingredients. Divide the mixture between the prepared baking trays.
3. Lower them into the drawers (without crisper plates).
4. Select zone 1 and pair it with "BAKE" at 180°C for 20 minutes. Select "MATCH" followed by the "START/STOP" button.
5. Bon appétit!

Per Serving:

Calories: 252g / Fat: 12.9g / Carbs: 19g / Fibre: 6.1g / Protein: 21.7g

Colorful Vegan Fritters

Prep time: 15 minutes / Cook time: 18 minutes / Serves 4

Ingredients

- 400g courgette, grated
- 200g sweet corn kernels, frozen and thawed
- 1 small onion, chopped
- 200g quick-cooking oats
- 1/2 tsp baking powder
- 2 tbsp flaxseed meal   • 100g tofu, crumbled
- 1/2 tsp dried dill   • 1 tsp paprika
- Sea salt and ground black pepper, to taste
- 1 tbsp olive oil

Instructions

1. Insert crisper plates in both drawers. Spray the crisper plates with nonstick cooking oil.
2. Mix the courgette with 1 teaspoon of coarse sea salt in a colander; let it sit for about 15 minutes; after that, squeeze out the excess moisture using tea towels.
3. Thoroughly combine the courgette with the remaining ingredients. Shape the mixture into small patties and arrange them in both drawers.
4. Select zone 1 and pair it with "AIR FRY" at 190°C for 18 minutes. Select "MATCH" followed by the "START/STOP" button.
5. When zone 1 time reaches 8 minutes, turn the courgette fritters over and reinsert the drawers to resume cooking.
6. Bon appétit!

Per Serving:

Calories: 390g / Fat: 15.2g / Carbs: 51g / Fibre: 10.7g / Protein: 18.1g

Mushroom and Tomato Burrito

Prep time: 10 minutes / Cook time: 16 minutes / Serves 4

Ingredients

* 500g brown mushrooms, halved
* 400g cherry tomatoes
* 2 tsp olive oil   • 1 tsp garlic granules
* 1 tsp dried oregano
* 1 tsp red pepper flakes
* Sea salt and ground black pepper, to taste
* 4 large tortillas
* 200g chickpeas, rinsed and drained
* 4 tbsp mayonnaise

Instructions

1. Toss the mushrooms and tomatoes with olive oil and spices. Add the mushrooms to the zone 1 drawer and tomatoes to the zone 2 drawer.
2. Select zone 1 and pair it with "ROAST" at 200°C for 10 minutes. Select zone 2 and pair it with "ROAST" at 180°C for 10 minutes. Select "SYNC" followed by the "START/STOP" button.
3. At the halfway point, toss your food and reinsert the drawers to resume cooking.
4. Assemble your burrito with tortillas, roasted mushrooms, tomatoes, chickpeas, and mayonnaise; wrap four burritos.
5. Use "REHEAT" mode to bake your burritos at 180°C for 6 minutes, until warmed through.

Per Serving:

Calories: 526g / Fat: 15.8g / Carbs: 79g / Fibre: 10.2g / Protein: 20.3g

Keto Seafood Salad

Prep time: 10 minutes / Cook time: 15 minutes / Serves 5

Ingredients

* 600g raw shrimp, peeled, tails on
* 400g bell peppers, deseeded and halved
* Sea salt and ground black pepper, to taste
* 1 large tomato, diced
* 1 small cucumber, sliced
* 2 spring onions, sliced
* 2 tbsp extra-virgin olive oil
* 1 tbsp fresh lemon juice

Instructions

1. Insert crisper plates in both drawers. Spray crisper plates with nonstick cooking oil.
2. Toss your shrimp and bell peppers with 1 tablespoon of olive oil and spices.
3. Place your shrimp in the zone 1 drawer and bell peppers in the zone 2 drawer.
4. Select zone 1 and pair it with "AIR FRY" at 190°C for 8 minutes. Select zone 2 and pair it with "ROAST" at 195°C for 15 minutes. Select "SYNC" followed by the "START/STOP" button.
5. At the halfway point, stir your food to promote even cooking and reinsert the drawers to resume cooking.
6. Cut the peppers into strips.
7. Toss your shrimp and pepper strips with the other ingredients. Devour!

Per Serving:

Calories: 206g / Fat: 7.5g / Carbs: 7.9g / Fibre: 1.6g / Protein: 25.8g

CHAPTER 7 : APPETIZERS & SNACKS

Potato Cakes with Spicy Sauce

Prep time: 35 minutes / Cook time: 25 minutes / Serves 4

Ingredients
- 600g potatoes, grated
- 1 small leek, chopped
- 1 large egg, beaten
- 20g oat flour
- 1 tsp paprika
- 1 tbsp olive oil
- Sea salt and ground black pepper, to taste
- Spicy Sauce:
- 100ml tomato sauce
- 50ml mayonnaise
- 1 chilli pepper, deseeded and finely chopped
- 1 tsp cayenne pepper

Instructions
1. Insert crisper plates in both drawers. Spray the crisper plates with nonstick cooking oil.
2. Use a food processor or a box grater to grate your potatoes; transfer them to a large bowl of very cold water. Let it sit for about 30 minutes.
3. Drain your potatoes and combine them with the remaining ingredients. Shape the mixture into small patties and arrange them in both drawers.
4. Select zone 1 and pair it with "AIR FRY" at 185°C for 25 minutes. Select "MATCH" followed by the "START/STOP" button.
5. When zone 1 time reaches 8 minutes, turn the potato cakes over and reinsert the drawers to resume cooking.
6. Meanwhile, mix all the Ingredients for the sauce. Serve the potato cakes with the sauce on the side.
7. Bon appétit!

Per Serving:
Calories: 293g / Fat: 10.4g / Carbs: 44g / Fibre: 5.6g / Protein: 7.3g

Colorful Vegetable Skewers

Prep time: 5 minutes / Cook time: 20 minutes / Serves 4

Ingredients
- 2 small onions, quartered
- 4 bell peppers, deseeded and sliced
- 1 medium aubergine, sliced
- 1 medium courgette, cut into thick slices
- 100g cherry tomatoes
- Sea salt and ground black pepper, to taste
- 1 tbsp Italian spice mix
- 1 tbsp olive oil
- 1 tsp balsamic vinegar
- 1 tbsp maple syrup

Instructions
1. Toss all the Ingredients until vegetables are well coated on all sides.
2. Alternately thread the vegetables onto the skewers until you run out of the ingredients.
3. Then, add the vegetables to the zone 1 and 2 drawers.
4. Select zone 1 and pair it with "ROAST" at 180°C for 20 minutes. Select "MATCH" followed by the "START/STOP" button.
5. At the halfway point, turn the skewers over and reinsert the drawers to resume cooking.
6. Bon appétit!

Per Serving:
Calories: 153g / Fat: 4.1g / Carbs: 28.7g / Fibre: 6.9g / Protein: 4.1g

Stuffed Mushroom Bites

Prep time: 10 minutes / Cook time: 15 minutes / Serves 6

Ingredients
- 12 button mushrooms
- 50g butter
- 200g tofu, pressed and crumbled
- 1 shallot, chopped
- 1 garlic clove, minced
- 1 tsp cayenne pepper
- 1 tbsp fresh parsley leaves, chopped
- 2 tbsp chives, chopped
- Sea salt and ground black pepper, to taste

Instructions
1. Pat the mushrooms dry with paper towels and

remove the stems; chop the stems and reserve.

2. Mix the mushroom stems with the other ingredients. Stir to combine and divide the filling between portobello mushrooms.

3. Place the stuffed mushrooms in both drawers and brush them with olive oil.

4. Select zone 1 and pair it with "ROAST" at 180°C for 15 minutes. Select "MATCH" followed by the "START/STOP" button.

5. Bon appétit!

Per Serving:

Calories: 163g / Fat: 13.7g / Carbs: 5.4g / Fibre: 1.9g / Protein: 7.1g

Sticky Chipolata Bites

Prep time: 5 minutes / Cook time: 15 minutes / Serves 6

Ingredients

* 600g mini chipolatas, casing removed
* 100ml BBQ sauce • 1 tbsp olive oil, divided

Instructions

1. Toss mini chipolatas with BBQ sauce and olive oil.

2. Add mini chipolatas to both drawers.

3. Select zone 1 and pair it with "AIR FRY" at 200°C for 15 minutes. Select "MATCH" followed by the "START/STOP" button.

4. Serve sticky chipolata bites with toothpicks and enjoy!

Per Serving:

Calories: 366g / Fat: 31.1g / Carbs: 9.2g / Fibre: 0.2g / Protein: 12.1g

Spicy Sticky Meatballs

Prep time: 10 minutes / Cook time: 20 minutes / Serves 6

Ingredients

* Meatballs:
* 400g pack of low-fat sausage
* 100g porridge oats
* 80g parmesan cheese, grated
* 2 spring onions, chopped
* 2 cloves garlic, minced
* A small handful of parsley, chopped

* Sauce:
* 2 tbsp soy sauce • 1 tbsp maple syrup
* Sea salt and ground black pepper, to taste
* 1 tbsp olive oil

Instructions

1. In a mixing bowl, thoroughly combine all the Ingredients for the meatballs. Mould the mixture into equal balls.

2. Select zone 1 and pair it with "AIR FRY" at 185°C for 20 minutes. Select "MATCH" to duplicate settings across both zones. Press the "START/STOP" button.

3. Meanwhile, mix all the Ingredients for the sauce.

4. At the halfway point, turn the meatballs over and drizzle them with the sauce; reinsert the drawers to resume cooking.

5. Serve meatballs with cocktail sticks.

6. Bon appétit!

Per Serving:

Calories: 377g / Fat: 22.5g / Carbs: 17.6g / Fibre: 2g / Protein: 25.9g

Cheesy Corn on the Cob

Prep time: 5 minutes / Cook time: 15 minutes / Serves 4

Ingredients

* 4 ears corn on the cob, halved
* 40g butter, room temperature
* 40g parmesan cheese, grated
* 1 tsp dried parsley flakes
* Flaky sea salt and ground black pepper, to taste

Instructions

1. In a small mixing bowl, thoroughly combine the butter, cheese, parsley, sea salt, and black pepper. Cut 8 pieces of tin foil and place 1/2 of the cob on each piece.

2. Transfer the packets to the cooking basket.

3. Select zone 1 and pair it with "BAKE" at 190°C for 15 minutes. Select "MATCH" followed by the "START/STOP" button.

4. At the halfway point, top your corn with the cheese mixture; reinsert the drawer to continue cooking.

5. Serve warm and enjoy!

Per Serving:
Calories: 242g / Fat: 11.9g / Carbs: 31.9g /
Fibre: 3.7g / Protein: 7.3g

Spicy Vegetarian "Wings"

Prep time: 10 minutes / Cook time: 20 minutes
/ Serves 5

Ingredients

- 100g parmesan cheese, grated
- 50g bread crumbs
- 1 tbsp olive oil
- 50ml hot sauce
- 1 tsp cayenne pepper
- 1 tsp garlic granules
- Sea salt and ground black pepper, to taste
- 1kg cauliflower florets

Instructions

1. Insert the crisper plates in both drawers and spray them with cooking oil.
2. Thoroughly combine the cheese, bread crumbs, olive oil, hot sauce, and spices.
3. Dip the cauliflower florets into the cheese mixture until they are well coated on all sides. Arrange them on the prepared crisper plates.
4. Select zone 1 and pair it with "ROAST" at 200°C for 20 minutes. Select "MATCH" to duplicate settings across both zones. Press the "START/STOP" button.
5. After 10 minutes, turn the wings over and reinsert the drawers to continue cooking.
6. Bon appétit!

Per Serving:
Calories: 188g / Fat: 9.2g / Carbs: 17.9g /
Fibre: 4.3g / Protein: 10.4g

Classic Bean Croquettes

Prep time: 10 minutes / Cook time: 20 minutes
/ Serves 5

Ingredients

- 400g canned pinto beans, drained and rinsed
- 200g quinoa, soaked overnight and rinsed
- 1 medium courgette, peeled
- 1 small leek
- 2 garlic cloves, peeled
- 2 tbsp hot sauce
- 100g instant oats

Instructions

1. Insert the crisper plates in both drawers and spray them with cooking oil.
2. Blend all the Ingredients in your food processor. Shape the mixture into 8 balls and lower them into both drawers.
3. Select zone 1 and pair it with "AIR FRY" at 185°C for 20 minutes. Select "MATCH" to duplicate settings across both zones. Press the "START/STOP" button.
4. When zone 1 time reaches 10 minutes, turn the croquettes over and reinsert the drawers to continue cooking.
5. Serve warm croquettes with the sauce for dipping and enjoy!

Per Serving:
Calories: 310g / Fat: 4.3g / Carbs: 55.3g /
Fibre: 9.3g / Protein: 13.4g

Crispy Maple Wings

Prep time: 10 minutes / Cook time: 33 minutes
/ Serves 4

Ingredients

- 800g chicken wings, drumettes & flats
- 1 tbsp sesame oil
- 1 tbsp corn flour
- 1 tsp red pepper flakes
- 1 tsp garlic granules
- Sea salt and ground black pepper, to taste
- 2 tbsp Worcestershire sauce
- 2 tbsp maple syrup

Instructions

1. Insert crisper plates in both drawers. Spray the crisper plates with nonstick cooking oil.
2. Toss chicken wings with the other ingredients. Divide the chicken wings between both drawers.
3. Select zone 1 and pair it with "AIR FRY" at 200°C for 33 minutes. Select "MATCH" followed by the "START/STOP" button.
4. Cook until the tops of the wings are starting to char a little.
5. Bon appétit!

Per Serving:
Calories: 327g / Fat: 10.5g / Carbs: 11.1g /
Fibre: 0.3g / Protein: 44.3g

Spicy Cauli Bites

Prep time: 10 minutes / Cook time: 20 minutes / Serves 5

Ingredients
- 1kg cauliflower florets
- 50ml hot sauce
- 1 tbsp olive oil
- Sea salt and ground black pepper, to taste

Instructions
1. Insert the crisper plates in both drawers and spray them with cooking oil.
2. Toss cauliflower florets with the hot sauce, olive oil, salt, and black pepper. Arrange cauliflower florets on the prepared crisper plates.
3. Select zone 1 and pair it with "ROAST" at 190°C for 20 minutes. Select "MATCH" to duplicate settings across both zones. Press the "START/STOP" button.
4. Bon appétit!

Per Serving:
Calories: 77g / Fat: 3.3g / Carbs: 10.1g / Fibre: 4g / Protein: 3.9g

Spicy Marinated Ribs

Prep time: 5 minutes + marinating time / Cook time: 40 minutes / Serves 4

Ingredients
- 1kg baby back pork ribs
- 2 tbsp Worcestershire sauce
- 50ml tomato ketchup
- 2 tbsp brown sugar
- 1 tbsp sweet chilli sauce
- Sea salt and ground black pepper, to taste

Instructions
1. Add the ribs along with the remaining Ingredients to a ceramic bowl; cover the bowl and allow the ribs to marinate for approximately 2 hours in your fridge. Reserve the marinade.
2. Arrange the ribs in two roasting trays and lower them into both drawers.
3. Select zone 1 and pair it with "AIR FRY" at 180°C for 40 minutes. Select "MATCH" to duplicate settings across both zones. Press the "START/STOP" button.
4. At the halfway point, turn the ribs over and baste them with the reserved marinade; reinsert the drawers to resume cooking.
5. Bon appétit!

Per Serving:
Calories: 377g / Fat: 14.1g / Carbs: 6.9g / Fibre: 0.2g / Protein: 52g

Shrimp Roll-Ups

Prep time: 5 minutes / Cook time: 20 minutes / Serves 8

Ingredients
- 8 king prawns
- 1 egg, beaten
- 2 x 250g packs of croissant dough
- 1 tbsp yellow mustard
- 2 tbsp tomato puree

Instructions
1. Add king prawns to both drawers. Select zone 1 and pair it with "AIR FRY" at 200°C for 10 minutes. Select "MATCH" followed by the "START/STOP" button.
2. Unroll the croissant packs. Place a king prawn on the wide end of each triangle croissant; add mustard and tomato puree, and roll them up. Arrange on two baking sheets and brush each croissant with beaten egg.
3. Select zone 1 and pair it with "BAKE" at 180°C for 10 minutes or until golden. Select "MATCH" followed by the "START/STOP" button.
4. Devour!

Per Serving:
Calories: 207g / Fat: 4.4g / Carbs: 33.5g / Fibre: 1.3g / Protein: 6.3g

Lemony Crab Sticks

Prep time: 10 minutes / Cook time: 15 minutes / Serves 4

Ingredients
- 600g crab sticks, cut into bite-sized pieces
- 2 tbsp fresh lemon juice
- 2 tsp sunflower oil
- 1 tsp garlic granules
- 1 tbsp fresh dill, chopped
- 1 tbsp fresh basil, chopped

Instructions

1. Insert crisper plates in both drawers and spray them with cooking oil.
2. Toss crab sticks with the other Ingredients and place them on crisper plates.
3. Select zone 1 and pair it with "AIR FRY" at 160°C for 15 minutes. Select "MATCH" to duplicate settings across both zones. Press the "START/STOP" button.
4. Shake the drawers halfway through the cooking time to ensure even cooking.
5. Devour!

Per Serving:

Calories: 158g / Fat: 4.1g / Carbs: 1.7g / Fibre: 0.4g / Protein: 27.5g

Twisted Falafel with Vegetables

Prep time: 10 minutes / Cook time: 20 minutes / Serves 5

Ingredients

- 400g canned chickpeas, drained and rinsed
- 1 large courgette, peeled
- 1 large carrot, peeled
- 1 small leek   • 2 garlic cloves, peeled
- 1 medium bell pepper, deseeded
- 1 chili pepper, deseeded
- 4 tbsp tomato puree

Instructions

1. Insert the crisper plates in both drawers and spray them with cooking oil.
2. Mix all the Ingredients in your food processor or a high-speed blender. Shape the mixture into 10 balls and lower them into both drawers.
3. Select zone 1 and pair it with "AIR FRY" at 185°C for 20 minutes. Select "MATCH" to duplicate settings across both zones. Press the "START/STOP" button.
4. When zone 1 time reaches 10 minutes, turn the falafel balls over and reinsert the drawers to continue cooking.
5. Serve warm falafel balls with toothpicks and enjoy!

Per Serving:

Calories: 233g / Fat: 8.8g / Carbs: 31.8g /

Fibre: 8.2g / Protein: 8.6g

Teriyaki Broccoli Florets

Prep time: 10 minutes / Cook time: 15 minutes / Serves 5

Ingredients

- 1kg broccoli florets   • 50ml soy sauce
- 20ml mirin   • 1 tbsp honey
- 1 tbsp olive oil   • 1 tbsp soy sauce
- Sea salt and ground black pepper, to taste

Instructions

1. Insert the crisper plates in both drawers and spray them with cooking oil.
2. Toss broccoli florets with the other ingredients. Arrange broccoli florets on the prepared crisper plates.
3. Select zone 1 and pair it with "ROAST" at 180°C for 15 minutes. Select "MATCH" to duplicate settings across both zones. Press the "START/STOP" button.
4. Bon appétit!

Per Serving:

Calories: 133g / Fat: 4g / Carbs: 18.8g / Fibre: 5.5g / Protein: 7.7g

Paprika Chicharrones

Prep time: 10 minutes + chilling time / Cook time: 13 minutes / Serves 9

Ingredients

- 600g pork skin
- 1 tbsp smoked paprika
- 1 tsp garlic granules
- 2 tbsp lemon juice
- 3 tbsp Worcestershire sauce
- Sea salt and ground black pepper, to taste

Instructions

1. Rub pork skins with the other ingredients; place in your refrigerator overnight.
2. Cut the crackling with kitchen scissors (any shape you like).
3. Now, place the pork skin in the cooking basket.
4. Select zone 1 and pair it with "AIR FRY" at 200°C for 13 minutes. Select "MATCH"

followed by the "START/STOP" button.

5. When zone 1 time reaches 6 minutes, shake the basket and reinsert the drawers to continue cooking. Enjoy!

Per Serving:

Calories: 150g / Fat: 70.5g / Carbs: 2.3g / Fibre: 0.5g / Protein: 17.3g

Vegan Asparagus Bites

Prep time: 10 minutes / Cook time: 10 minutes / Serves 6

Ingredients

- 800g asparagus spears, trimmed
- 100g raw sunflower seeds
- 30g nutritional yeast
- 1/2 tsp onion powder
- 1/2 tsp garlic granules
- 1/4 tsp dried dill weed
- Sea salt and ground black pepper, to taste
- 1 tbsp sesame oil

Instructions

1. Pat dry the asparagus with tea towels and cut off the tips. Using your blender or food processor, blend the sunflower seeds, nutritional yeast, and spices into a vegan sauce.
2. Add the asparagus spears to both drawers and brush them with sesame oil.
3. Select zone 1 and pair it with "AIR FRY" at 200°C for 10 minutes. Select "MATCH" followed by the "START/STOP" button.
4. At the halfway point, top your asparagus with the sauce; reinsert the drawers to resume cooking.
5. Devour!

Per Serving:

Calories: 157g / Fat: 11.1g / Carbs: 10.5g / Fibre: 4.7g / Protein: 7.8g

Crispy Brussels Sprouts

Prep time: 10 minutes / Cook time: 13 minutes / Serves 6

Ingredients

- 800g whole Brussels sprouts
- 2 tbsp corn flour
- 2 tbsp butter, melted

- 2 tbsp soy sauce
- 2 tbsp maple syrup
- Sea salt and black pepper, to taste

Instructions

1. Tip Brussels sprouts into two roasting tins and toss them with the other ingredients.
2. Select zone 1 and pair it with "ROAST" at 190°C for 13 minutes. Select "MATCH" to duplicate settings across both zones. Press the "START/STOP" button.
3. When zone 1 time reaches 6 minutes, shake the basket and reinsert the drawers to continue cooking.
4. Bon appétit!

Per Serving:

Calories: 137g / Fat: 5.3g / Carbs: 19.5g / Fibre: 5.4g / Protein: 5.1g

Cheesy Mushroom Bites

Prep time: 10 minutes / Cook time: 14 minutes / Serves 6

Ingredients

- 600g button mushrooms, cleaned and stems removed
- 2 large eggs
- 1 tsp onion powder
- 1 tsp garlic granules
- 1 tsp dried oregano
- 1 tbsp olive oil
- Sea salt and ground black pepper, to taste
- 100g plain flour
- 50g crushed tortilla chips
- 50g Parmesan cheese, grated

Instructions

1. Insert crisper plates in both drawers. Spray crisper plates with nonstick cooking oil.
2. Pat the mushrooms dry using tea (paper) towels.
3. Now, make the breading station: Beat the eggs until pale and frothy. In a separate shallow dish, mix the spices and flour. In a third shallow dish, thoroughly combine the crushed tortilla chips with Parmesan cheese and olive oil.
4. Dip the mushrooms in the egg, then, dust your mushrooms with the flour mixture. Roll them over the Parmesan mixture, pressing to adhere.
5. Arrange the prepared mushrooms on the crisper plates.

6. Select zone 1 and pair it with "AIR FRY" at 190°C for 14 minutes. Select "MATCH" to duplicate settings across both zones. Press the "START/STOP" button.
7. When zone 1 time reaches 6 minutes, turn the mushrooms over using silicone-tipped tongs. Reinsert the drawers to continue cooking. Enjoy!

Per Serving:
Calories: 193g / Fat: 7g / Carbs: 23.3g / Fibre: 2.6g / Protein: 11.1g

Herb Potato Bites

Prep time: 5 minutes / Cook time: 20 minutes / Serves 4

Ingredients
- 1kg potatoes, peeled and cut into wedges (Maris Piper or Desiré potatoes)
- 1 tbsp fresh cilantro leaves, chopped
- 1 tbsp fresh parsley leaves, chopped
- 1 tbsp fresh rosemary leaves, chopped
- 1 tbsp olive oil
- 1 tsp red pepper flakes
- Sea salt and ground black pepper, to taste

Instructions
1. Toss the potatoes with the other ingredients. Place the potatoes in the cooking basket.
2. Select zone 1 and pair it with "ROAST" at 200°C for 20 minutes. Select "MATCH" followed by the "START/STOP" button.
3. Cook until slightly charred and enjoy!

Per Serving:
Calories: 223g / Fat: 3.6g / Carbs: 43.3g / Fibre: 5.6g / Protein: 5.1g

Spicy Green Bean Chips

Prep time: 10 minutes / Cook time: 12 minutes / Serves 5

Ingredients
- 1 kg green beans, trimmed
- 1 tbsp olive oil, divided
- 1 tsp chilli powder
- 1 tsp garlic granules
- Sea salt and black pepper, to taste

Instructions
1. Toss green beans with olive oil and spices. Add green beans to both drawers (with a crisper plate inserted).
2. Select zone 1 and pair it with "AIR FRY" at 200°C for 12 minutes. Select "MATCH" followed by the "START/STOP" button.
3. When zone 1 time reaches 5 minutes, shake the drawers and toss green beans with Parmesan cheese. Reinsert the drawers to continue cooking.
4. Devour!

Per Serving:
Calories: 86g / Fat: 3.1g / Carbs: 13.9g / Fibre: 5.5g / Protein: 3.6g

Glazed Root Vegetables

Prep time: 10 minutes / Cook time: 20 minutes / Serves 6

Ingredients
- 300g carrots, cut into sticks
- 200g parsnips, cut into sticks
- 200g red beets, peeled, cut into sticks
- 2 tbsp butter, melted
- 2 tbsp sherry vinegar
- 1 tsp cayenne pepper
- Sea salt and black pepper, to taste
- 2 tbsp maple syrup

Instructions
1. Tip the vegetables into two roasting tins and toss them with butter, sherry vinegar, cayenne pepper, salt, and black pepper.
2. Select zone 1 and pair it with "ROAST" at 180°C for 20 minutes. Select "MATCH" to duplicate settings across both zones. Press the "START/STOP" button.
3. When zone 1 time reaches 10 minutes, toss the vegetables with maple syrup and reinsert the drawers to continue cooking.
4. Bon appétit!

Per Serving:
Calories: 116g / Fat: 4.2g / Carbs: 19g / Fibre: 4.2g / Protein: 1.6g

CHAPTER 8 : DESSERTS

Autumn Crisp with Walnuts

Prep time: 10 minutes / Cook time: 30 minutes / Serves 6

Ingredients

- 2 tsp butter, room temperature
- 1 medium apple, cored and diced
- 6 plums, stoned and halved
- 2 tbsp lime juice
- 60g golden caster sugar
- 2 tbsp cornstarch
- 1 tsp ground cinnamon
- A pinch of sea salt
- Topping:
- 40ml coconut oil, melted
- 100g walnuts, chopped
- 100g quick-cooking oats
- 100g honey
- 1 tsp vanilla extract

Instructions

1. Grease two baking trays with butter and set them aside.
2. Toss your fruits with lime juice, golden caster sugar, cornstarch, cinnamon, and salt. Arrange the fruits in the prepared baking trays.
3. In a bowl, thoroughly combine all the topping Ingredients until a crumb-like texture has formed. Scatter the topping mixture all over the fruits.
4. Lower the baking trays into the cooking basket.
5. Select zone 1 and pair it with "BAKE" at 170°C for 30 minutes. Select "MATCH" followed by the "START/STOP" button.
6. Devour!

Per Serving:
Calories: 334g / Fat: 19.2g / Carbs: 42.5g / Fibre: 3.3g / Protein: 3.7g

Star Anise Cupcakes

Prep time: 10 minutes / Cook time: 17 minutes / Serves 8

Ingredients

- 2 large eggs
- 300g apple sauce
- 100g coconut oil, room temperature
- 200g self-raising plain flour
- 200g brown sugar
- A pinch of sea salt
- 1/4 tsp ground anise
- 1/4 tsp ground cinnamon

Instructions

1. Preheat the Ninja Foodi to 160°C for 5 minutes. Spray 8 muffin cases with nonstick oil.
2. In a separate mixing bowl, whisk the eggs until pale and frothy. Gradually stir in apple sauce and coconut oil; mix until everything is well incorporated.
3. In another bowl, thoroughly combine the dry ingredients.
4. Slowly and gradually, add the dry Ingredients to the liquid mixture; mix again to combine. Spoon the batter into the prepared muffin cases. Place 4 muffin cases in each drawer.
5. Select zone 1 and pair it with "BAKE" at 170°C for 17 minutes. Select "MATCH" followed by the "START/STOP" button.
6. Allow your muffins to rest on a cooling rack for about 10 minutes before unmolding and serving.

Per Serving:
Calories: 217g / Fat: 1.5g / Carbs: 46g / Fibre: 1.3g / Protein: 4.8g

Classic Brownie

Prep time: 12 minutes / Cook time: 20 minutes / Serves 10

Ingredients

- 200g dark chocolate (70-85% cacao solids), cut into chunks
- 150g unsalted butter, room temperature
- 150g brown sugar
- 2 large eggs, lightly beaten
- 200g oat flour
- 1 tsp ground cinnamon
- 1 tsp pure vanilla paste
- 1/2 tsp ground cloves

Instructions

1. Grease two baking tins with cooking oil.
2. Melt the chocolate, butter and sugar in your microwave. (You can also use a small saucepan and melt the Ingredients at low temperature for about 2 minutes; keep a close eye on it).
3. Fold in the eggs and beat again to combine well. Stir in the other Ingredients and mix until everything is well combined.
4. Select zone 1 and pair it with "BAKE" at 170°C for 20 minutes. Select "MATCH" followed by the "START/STOP" button.
5. Allow your brownie to rest on a cooling rack for about 10 minutes before cutting and serving. Devour!

Per Serving:
Calories: 350g / Fat: 19.5g / Carbs: 37.6g / Fibre: 3.6g / Protein: 6.3g

Apple & Cinnamon Pie Samosas

Prep time: 12 minutes / Cook time: 14 minutes / Serves 10

Ingredients

- 450g sheets filo pastry
- 4 medium apples, peeled, cored and chopped
- 100g caster sugar
- 1 tsp cinnamon powder
- 100g raisins

Instructions

1. Cut the sheets of filo pastry in thirds lengthways. Divide the filling between pastry strips; fold over to form triangular parcels. Repeat until you run out of ingredients.
2. Grease two baking tins with cooking oil.
3. Select zone 1 and pair it with "BAKE" at 175°C for 14 minutes. Select "MATCH" followed by the "START/STOP" button.
4. Dust with powdered sugar, if desired. Enjoy!

Per Serving:
Calories: 358g / Fat: 17.7g / Carbs: 48.6g / Fibre: 3g / Protein: 3.8g

Mini Blackberry Cheesecakes

Prep time: 30 minutes / Cook time: 13 minutes / Serves 6

Ingredients

- 100g powdered sugar
- 150g butter, room temperature
- 150g plain flour
- 100g oat flour
- 1 tbsp flaxseed meal
- A pinch of ground cinnamon
- 1/4 tsp sea salt
- 250g mascarpone cheese, room temperature
- 1 tsp vanilla paste
- 200g frozen blackberries

Instructions

1. Beat the sugar with butter until well combined. Add in the flour, flaxseed meal, cinnamon, and salt.
2. Press the mixture into lightly greased ramekins.
3. Select zone 1 and pair it with "BAKE" at 175°C for 13 minutes. Select "MATCH" followed by the "START/STOP" button.
4. Then, make the cheesecake topping by mixing the cheese, vanilla, and 100 grams of mixed berries. Place this topping over the crust; place your cheesecake in the freezer for a further 30 minutes.
5. Garnish with the remaining blackberries and serve well-chilled. Devour!

Per Serving:
Calories: 488g / Fat: 23g / Carbs: 51.9g / Fibre: 4.7g / Protein: 19.2g

Authentic Churros

Prep time: 12 minutes / Cook time: 15 minutes / Serves 6

Ingredients

- 230ml water
- 75g unsalted butter, cold, cut into cubes
- 2 tbsp granulated sugar
- 125g plain flour
- 1 tsp vanilla extract
- 1/4 tsp salt
- 2 large eggs
- Cinnamon Sugar Coating:
- 100g granulated sugar
- 1 tsp ground cinnamon

Instructions

1. In a medium saucepan, bring the water, butter, and sugar to a simmer. Let it simmer until the butter has fully melted; heat off.
2. To make the choux pastry, tip in the flour, vanilla, and salt; whisk vigorously to combine well. Return the mixture to the heat and let it simmer until a smooth ball forms.
3. Then, add the eggs, one at a time, and continue mixing using an electric mixer. This pastry should be slightly sticky and tick
4. Add the choux pastry to a piping bag fitted with an open star tip. Pipe your churros onto two lightly greased baking trays. Brush the pastry with nonstick oil.
5. Select zone 1 and pair it with "BAKE" at 180°C for 15 minutes. Select "MATCH" followed by the "START/STOP" button.
6. Meanwhile, mix the Ingredients for the cinnamon sugar coating. Toss warm churros in the coating mixture and enjoy!

Per Serving:
Calories: 248g / Fat: 8.8g / Carbs: 35.5g / Fibre: 0.7g / Protein: 4.7g

Easy Almond Fudge

Prep time: 12 minutes / Cook time: 18 minutes / Serves 10

- Ingredients
- Cake:
- 200g dark chocolate (70-85% cacao solids), cut into chunks
- 150g unsalted butter, room temperature
- 40g cocoa powder
- 1 large egg
- 180g brown sugar
- 60g oat flour
- 1/2 tsp ground cloves
- 1/2 tsp ground cinnamon
- 60g almonds, chopped
- Topping:
- 200ml tin condensed milk
- 150g almond butter, smooth
- 150g dark chocolate (70-85% cacao solids), cut into chunks

Instructions

1. Butter two baking tins and set them aside.
2. Microwave the chocolate, butter, and cocoa powder. Whisk the mixture until it has fully melted.
3. In a mixing dish, beat the egg with brown sugar until frothy; add the other Ingredients for the cake and mix to combine. Fold in the chocolate mixture and stir until everything is well incorporated.
4. Select zone 1 and pair it with "BAKE" at 180°C for 18 minutes. Select "MATCH" followed by the "START/STOP" button.
5. Meanwhile, set an ovenproof bowl over a pan of simmering water. Whisk the topping Ingredients in the bowl until everything is fully melted.
6. Afterwards, spread the topping mixture over the cooled fudge base. Enjoy!

Per Serving:
Calories: 540g / Fat: 38.4g / Carbs: 42.2g / Fibre: 5.3g / Protein: 6.4g

Cinnamon Baked Pears

Prep time: 10 minutes / Cook time: 15 minutes / Serves 5

Ingredients

- 150g quick-cooking oats
- 150g almonds, chopped
- 1/2 tsp grated nutmeg
- 1 tsp cinnamon powder
- 100ml honey
- 5 large pears, stems and seeds removed

Ingredients

1. In a mixing bowl, combine quick-cooking oats, almonds, nutmeg, cinnamon, and honey.
2. Divide the filling mixture between your pears and arrange them in the lightly greased cooking basket.
3. Select zone 1 and pair it with "BAKE" at 175°C for 15 minutes. Select "MATCH" followed by the "START/STOP" button.
4. Bon appétit!

Per Serving:
Calories: 355g / Fat: 14.6g / Carbs: 47.3g / Fibre: 0.8g / Protein: 4.2g

Mini Cream Cakes

Prep time: 10 minutes / Cook time: 25 minutes / Serves 6

Ingredients

- 100g butter, softened
- 1 large egg
- 150g golden caster sugar
- 1/2 tsp anise star, ground
- 1 vanilla pod, split lengthways and seeds scraped out
- 180g self-raising flour
- 1/2 tsp baking powder

Instructions

1. Lightly grease 6 custard cups with nonstick cooking oil.
2. Beat the butter and egg until pale and frothy. Then, add the sugar, anise, and vanilla, and mix to combine well.
3. Stir in the flour and baking powder; mix again to combine well. Divide the batter between the prepared custard cups.
4. Select zone 1 and pair it with "BAKE" at 160°C for 25 minutes. Select "MATCH" followed by the "START/STOP" button.
5. Bon appétit!

Per Serving:
Calories: 335g / Fat: 14.6g / Carbs: 47.3g / Fibre: 0.8g / Protein: 4.2g

Nutty Fruit Crumble

Prep time: 10 minutes / Cook time: 23 minutes / Serves 6

Ingredients

- 10 plums, stones, and sliced
- 1 medium pear, peeled, cored and sliced
- 1 tbsp lime juice
- 2 tbsp clear honey
- Crumble:
- 170g plain flour
- 100g brown sugar
- 100g coconut oil
- Serving:
- Clotted cream, to serve (optional)

Instructions

1. Grease two baking trays with cooking oil.
2. Toss your fruits with lime juice and honey. Arrange your fruits in the prepared baking trays.
3. Put plain flour and brown sugar in a bowl of your food processor. Now, add the cold coconut oil and mix until it looks like moist breadcrumbs.
4. Pour the crumb mix over the fruits, using a spatula to even out.
5. Lower the baking trays into both drawers.
6. Select zone 1 and pair it with "BAKE" at 170°C for 23 minutes. Select "MATCH" followed by the "START/STOP" button.
7. Devour!

Per Serving:
Calories: 340g / Fat: 1.2g / Carbs: 81.1g / Fibre: 6.6g / Protein: 5.2g

Chocolate Lover's Cakes

Prep time: 5 minutes / Cook time: 10 minutes / Serves 4

Ingredients

- 2 large bananas, peeled and mashed
- 4 eggs, beaten
- 1 tsp vanilla extract
- 1/2 tsp cinnamon powder
- 50ml honey
- 2 tbsp almond butter
- 60g oat flour
- 1 tsp baking powder
- 4 tbsp chocolate chips

Instructions

1. Mash bananas and eggs until frothy; add the other Ingredients and mix to combine well.
2. Divide the Ingredients between four ramekins and place them in the cooking basket.
3. Select zone 1 and pair it with "BAKE" at 180°C for 10 minutes. Select "MATCH" followed by the "START/STOP" button.
4. Devour!

Per Serving:

Calories: 386g / Fat: 11.9g / Carbs: 61.8g / Fibre: 4.6g / Protein: 9.5g

Cinnamon Apple Fritters

Prep time: 5 minutes / Cook time: 18 minutes / Serves 5

Ingredients

- 200g self-raising flour
- 1/2 tsp baking powder
- 1/2 tsp vanilla extract
- 1 tsp cinnamon powder
- A pinch of ground cloves
- A pinch of sea salt　　• 2 eggs
- 60g brown sugar　•　100ml full-fat milk
- 2 medium apples, cored and grated
- 2 tbsp vegetable oil

Instructions

1. Line both drawers with parchment paper.
2. In a mixing bowl, thoroughly combine the dry ingredients.
3. Then, separate the egg yolk from the egg white. Beat the egg yolk with brown sugar and milk. Beat the egg white until stiff peaks form.
4. Gradually add the egg white to the egg yolk mixture.
5. Add the liquid Ingredients to the dry ingredients; fold in the grated apples and stir to combine well.
6. Use a cookie scoop to create the dollops of batter and arrange them in both drawers. Drizzle your fritters with vegetable oil.
7. Select zone 1 and pair it with "AIR FRY" at 180°C for 18 minutes. Select "MATCH" followed by the "START/STOP" button.
8. Bon appétit!

Per Serving:

Calories: 313g / Fat: 8.8g / Carbs: 52.8g / Fibre: 2.8g / Protein: 6.9g

Easy Fluffy Cupcakes

Prep time: 15 minutes / Cook time: 18 minutes / Serves 6

Ingredients

- Cupcakes:
- 1 medium egg, beaten
- 1 tbsp butter, room temperature
- 200ml oat milk, unsweetened
- 250g old-fashioned rolled oats
- 1 tbsp chia seeds　　• 1 tsp baking powder
- 50ml clear honey　•　1 tsp ground cinnamon
- Serving:
- 100ml whipped cream

Instructions

1. Brush the inside of 6 muffin cases with cooking oil.
2. Thoroughly combine all the Ingredients for the cupcakes; now, spoon the mixture into the prepared muffin cases. Add the muffin cases to the drawers.
3. Select zone 1 and pair it with "BAKE" at 185°C for 18 minutes. Select "MATCH" to duplicate settings across both zones. Press the

"START/STOP" button.

4. Let your cupcakes cool for about 10 minutes before unmolding.

5. In the meantime, prepare your whipped cream.

6. To serve, scoop the whipped cream onto the cupcakes and enjoy!

Per Serving:

Calories: 273g / Fat: 9.9g / Carbs: 37.7g / Fibre: 5.2g / Protein: 9.9g

Mini Jam Flapjacks

Prep time: 10 minutes / Cook time: 16 minutes / Serves 8

Ingredients

- 1 tsp vegetable oil
- 2 eggs, beaten
- 100ml coconut milk
- 130g oat flour
- 250g plain flour
- 1 tsp baking powder
- 1/4 tsp sea salt
- A pinch of ground cinnamon
- 8 tbsp strawberry jam

Instructions

1. Grease 8 muffin cases with vegetable oil.

2. Beat the eggs with coconut milk until pale and frothy. Gradually stir in the flour baking powder, salt, and cinnamon; beat the mixture with an electric mixer to ensure no lumps are created.

3. Divide the batter between the prepared muffin cases.

4. Select zone 1 and pair it with "BAKE" at 180°C for 16 minutes. Select "MATCH" followed by the "START/STOP" button.

5. At the half point, dot over the strawberry jam and reinsert the drawers to continue cooking.

6. Bon appétit!

Per Serving:

Calories: 263g / Fat: 7.8g / Carbs: 39.7g / Fibre: 2.4g / Protein: 8.2g

Peanut Butter Cookies

Prep time: 15 minutes / Cook time: 15 minutes / Serves 8

Ingredients

- 100g plain flour
- 100g oat flour
- 1 tsp baking powder
- 120g honey
- 100g peanut butter, room temperature
- 1/2 tsp ground cinnamon powder
- 1 tsp vanilla extract
- 120ml almond milk
- 50g raisins

Instructions

1. Begin by preheating your Air Fryer to 180°C for 5 minutes.

2. In a mixing bowl, thoroughly combine the dry ingredients; mix until your mixture resembles breadcrumbs.

3. In another bowl, thoroughly combine all the wet ingredients. Add the wet mixture to the dry ingredients; fold in raisins and stir to combine well.

4. Shape the balls using an ice cream scoop; now, arrange the balls on the parchment-lined baking tins.

5. Select zone 1 and pair it with "BAKE" at 180°C for 15 minutes. Select "MATCH" followed by the "START/STOP" button.

6. Let your cookies cool for approximately 10 minutes before serving. Enjoy!

Per Serving:

Calories: 203g / Fat: 3.6g / Carbs: 38.7g / Fibre: 1.7g / Protein: 4.6g

Chocolate Explosion Cakes

Prep time: 10 minutes / Cook time: 20 minutes / Serves 8

Ingredients

- 130g dark chocolate, chopped
- 100g brown soft sugar
- 130g butter, plus extra to grease
- 1 tsp cinnamon powder
- 3 large eggs
- 1 tsp vanilla extract
- 70g plain flour

Instructions

1. Microwave chocolate chunks, brown sugar, and butter for about seconds until the mixture is uniform and smooth.
2. Now, stir in the remaining ingredients; whisk to combine well. Pour the batter into four lightly oiled ramekins.
3. Select zone 1 and pair it with "BAKE" at 170°C for 20 minutes. Select "MATCH" followed by the "START/STOP" button.
4. Devour!

Per Serving:

Calories: 316g / Fat: 21.9g / Carbs: 26.9g / Fibre: 2.2g / Protein: 3.4g

Caramel Bloomin' Apples

Prep time: 10 minutes / Cook time: 20 minutes / Serves 8

Ingredients

- 1 tbsp brown sugar
- 4 tbsp butter, melted
- 1/2 tsp ground cinnamon
- 1 tbsp honey
- 4 apples, sliced top off
- 8 chewy caramel squares

Instructions

1. Thoroughly combine the sugar, butter, cinnamon, and honey.
2. Use a melon baller or a teaspoon to core your apples. Create two deep, circular cuts around the centre of the apple.
3. Turn your apples over and make narrow cuts all the way around the apple; be careful not to cut through the core.
4. Add two caramel squares to each apple. Arrange them in the cooking basket.
5. Select zone 1 and pair it with "BAKE" at

170°C for 20 minutes. Select "MATCH" followed by the "START/STOP" button.
6. Bon appétit!

Per Serving:

Calories: 176g / Fat: 7g / Carbs: 28.3g / Fibre: 2.1g / Protein: 0.7g

Mini Autumn Pies

Prep time: 12 minutes / Cook time: 14 minutes / Serves 8

Ingredients

- 2 large apples, peeled, cored, and diced
- 60g brown sugar
- 1 tsp cinnamon
- 1/2 tsp nutmeg, preferably freshly grated
- 2 tbsp cornstarch
- 8 spring roll wrappers
- 2 tbsp coconut oil, melted

Instructions

1. In a mixing bowl, thoroughly combine the apples, brown sugar, cinnamon, nutmeg, and cornstarch.
2. Lay out the spring roll wrappers on a clean surface. Divide the apple mixture between the wrappers.
3. Fold your wrappers diagonally to form triangles, seal the edges, and brush them with coconut oil.
4. Line two baking tins with baking paper.
5. Select zone 1 and pair it with "BAKE" at 175°C for 14 minutes. Select "MATCH" followed by the "START/STOP" button.
6. Enjoy!

Per Serving:

Calories: 190g / Fat: 4g / Carbs: 35.8g / Fibre: 2.1g / Protein: 3.3g

28-Day Meal Plan

	Breakfast	Lunch	Dinner	Snack/Dessert
Day 1	Hash Brown Quiche Cups	BBQ Duck Wings	Hungarian Beef Goulash	Potato Cakes with Spicy Sauce
Day 2	Mini Pizza Tarlets	Peppercorn Chicken	Pork Hot Pot	Stuffed Mushroom Bites
Day 3	Baked Almond & Banana Porridge	Mexican-Style Chicken Meatloaf	Steak & Aubergine Salad	Sticky Chipolata Bites
Day 4	Colourful Egg Cups	Easy Turkey Enchiladas	Prawn & Cauliflower Salad	Cheesy Corn on the Cob
Day 5	Granola Raisin Bars	Roast Pork with Crackling	Pork Chop Melts	Classic Bean Croquettes
Day 6	Autumn Pumpkin Muffins	Beef Curry	BBQ Fish Tarts	Autumn Crisp with Walnuts
Day 7	Toasted Bread with Breakfast Sausages	Thanksgiving Roast Turkey	Pulled Pork Tacos	Star Anise Cupcakes
Day 8	Croissant French Toast	Hearty Cheeseburger Casserole	Easy Sticky Ribs	Classic Brownie
Day 9	Aromatic Banana Fritters	Easy Pork Burritos	Restaurant-Style Fish Fillets	Apple & Cinnamon Pie Samosas
Day 10	Spicy Bacon Omelette	Spicy Turkey Pasta Bake	Garlicky Prawns with Roasted Peppers	Lemony Crab Sticks
Day 11	The Best Sticky Bun Ever	Pork Carnitas	Seafood Jambalaya	Mini Blackberry Cheesecakes
Day 12	Winter Frittata with Bacon	Garlicky Halibut Steak with Asparagus	Beef Brisket Pot Roast	Authentic Churros
Day 13	Flapjacks with Golden Raisins	Sea Scallops with Mushrooms	Roast Fish Italian Style	Teriyaki Broccoli Florets
Day 14	Mixed Berry Muffins	Classic Chicken Risotto	Barbecued Pork Chops	Easy Almond Fudge
Day 15	Bacon & Egg Bap	Mediterranean-Style Roast Fish	Marinated Squid with Baby Carrots	Cinnamon Baked Pears

	Breakfast	Lunch	Dinner	Snack/Dessert
Day 16	Breakfast Pie with Bacon	Pork Fajitas	Spicy Peppery Meatloaves	Mini Cream Cakes
Day 17	Italian-Style Mini Frittata	Roast Loin of Pork with Herbs	Roast Fish with Chorizo	Nutty Fruit Crumble
Day 18	Superfood Quinoa Porridge	Turkey Traybake	Cheesy Halibut in a Parcel	Chocolate Lover's Cakes
Day 19	Cornbread Muffins	Seafood Conge	Sunday Roast	Cinnamon Apple Fritters
Day 20	Cinnamon Banana Bread Muffins	Authentic Beef Stroganoff	Spicy Sea Scallops with Roasted Leeks	Easy Fluffy Cupcakes
Day 21	Avocado Toast with Beans	Turkey Burgers	Sticky Gammon Steaks	Mini Jam Flapjacks
Day 22	Omelette with Spinach and Pancetta	Pork and Green Bean Casserole	Seafood Quinoa Pilau	Peanut Butter Cookies
Day 23	Baked Almond & Banana Porridge	Easy Chicken Frittata	Shrimp Tacos	Chocolate Explosion Cakes
Day 24	Toasted Bread with Breakfast Sausages	Chinese-Style Pork Medallions	Prawn and Tomato Sandwich	Caramel Bloomin' Apples
Day 25	Flapjacks with Golden Raisins	Baked Avocado Eggs with Shrimp	Sauerkraut with Pork Sausage	Mini Autumn Pies
Day 26	Italian-Style Mini Frittata	Cheesy Paprika Steak	Indian Fish Mappas	Glazed Root Vegetables
Day 27	Aromatic Banana Fritters	Tuna Steak with Broccoli	Zesty Shrimp with Courgette	Spicy Green Bean Chips
Day 28	Cornbread Muffins	Chicken Nuggets	Pork Sausage and Vegetable Traybake	Herb Potato Bites

INDEX

Printed in Great Britain
by Amazon

31945366R00046